D1029699

MATTHEW FONTAINE MAURY
THE PATHFINDER OF THE SEAS

MATTHEW FONTAINE MAURY

THE PATHFINDER OF THE SEAS

By
CHARLES LEE LEWIS

ℰ

ILLUSTRATED

AMS PRESS
NEW YORK

Reprinted from the edition of 1927, Annapolis
First AMS EDITION published 1969
Manufactured in the United States of America

Library of Congress Catalogue Card Number: 72-98638

AMS PRESS, INC.
New York, N.Y. 10003

TO MY WIFE
LOUISE QUARLES LEWIS

COMMANDER RICHARD EVELYN BYRD, U. S. NAVY (RETIRED)

Who has written the Foreword of this biography

FOREWORD

I believe that the most instructive form of reading is biography. In the story of a man's life one can see in quick review the struggle that man went through to attain or to fail to attain his heart's desire.

For the professional man, life stories of his colleagues and predecessors focus down to the particular problems of the profession. This is essentially the case with the story of a man like Maury. As a naval officer, Maury's work will always remain outstanding. He was one of our pioneer investigators of the geography of the sea and the physics of the air. And at the same time he never lost sight of the intrinsic needs of his Service.

Since travel in the present age has become so common Maury may be looked upon as one of our great benefactors. His professional work turned out to be of happily wide application, not only for the seafaring man, but for the flier.

As an inspirational character Maury was also a noteworthy American. His life was marked by that persistent industry peculiar to the successful research worker. There is little indication that he ever saw ahead of him immediate reward of any great size. But his toil was ever directly applied for the adventure of discovering something new or different in the maritime fields in which he worked.

Because I am soon to start on my own expedition towards the South Pole I am particularly interested in a letter Maury wrote under date of August 20, 1860, in which he said: "I have reason to believe that there is, about the South Pole, a comparatively mild climate. The unexplored regions there embrace an area equal in extent to about one-sixth of all the known land on the surface of the earth. I am quietly seeking to create in the minds of some an interest upon the subject, hoping thereby to foster a desire in right quarters for an Antarctic expedition."

RICHARD E. BYRD
Commander, U. S. Navy (Retired)

September 26, 1927

PUBLISHER'S STATEMENT

Measured by man's calendar it has been a long stretch of time since he first ventured forth in crude canoes on the waters skirting his early habitations.

The art of handling ships—seamanship and navigation—began before man could read or write; it was ships that first quickened his imagination and enabled him to measure his skill against Nature's elements and released him from the encirclement of small operations.

Western Europe and its civilization saved themselves from being pushed into the Atlantic by the flanking movement afforded by ships—increased knowledge of navigation.

No single individual has done more for his fellow man in lessening the hazards of navigation than has MATTHEW FONTAINE MAURY.

For the safe navigation of aircraft the world is waiting today for another MAURY. Aerology is in its infancy.

No other life of this distinguished naval officer and scientist has been published in America and the author has spent the greater part of four years in its preparation.

To Commander Byrd the author and the publisher are indebted for the Foreword.

To the Hydrographic Office, Navy Department, appreciation for assistance and advice rendered is expressed.

That MAURY's fame and honor may ever grow greater and that his life's work may be an inspiration for a future PATHFINDER OF THE AIR appears a sufficient reason for the publication of this biography by his brother officers of the NAVY.

UNITED STATES NAVAL INSTITUTE

September 27, 1927

PREFACE

This biography is based chiefly upon the Maury Papers, comprising letters, diaries, scientific notebooks, and other manuscripts, which were presented to the United States Government in 1912 by Maury's only living child, Mrs. Mary Maury Werth, and other descendants, and then deposited in the Division of Manuscripts, Library of Congress. Other valuable sources are the letter books, numbering many volumes, in the Office of the Superintendent of the United States Naval Observatory in Washington, and the official papers relating to Maury in the Navy Department Library. Miscellaneous Maury letters are to be found in the New York Public Library, the Public Library of the City of Boston, the United States Naval Academy Museum, the Peabody Institute Library of Baltimore, the Virginia State Library, the Virginia Historical Society Library, and the Yale University Library. Mrs. C. Alphonso Smith, Raleigh, North Carolina, has one Maury letter and some fifty others, written by contemporaries in reference to the Maury Testimonial which was presented to him in England after the Civil War. Of great importance, also, are Maury's own voluminous writings, and the numerous references to him in the periodicals and newspapers of his time.

For assistance in gathering material for this biography I wish to acknowledge my indebtedness to various members of the Maury family. In the first place, I wish to mention the "Life of Maury" by his daughter, Diana Fontaine Maury Corbin, which was of considerable help to me.   Of his living descendants, Mrs. James Parmelee, a granddaughter, of Washington, D. C., and Mrs. Matthew Fontaine Maury, Jr., a daughter-in-law, of Cincinnati, Ohio gave me much assistance.   Mrs. Werth of Richmond, Virginia, and her two daughters, Mrs. N. Montgomery Osborne of Norfolk, Virginia, and Mrs. Littleton Fitzgerald of Richmond, very patiently answered my numerous questions and furnished me interesting and very desirable information.   The list of all the other persons who have helped me, in one way or another, in the writing of this book would be too long to set down in a preface; but among the many I wish to single out by name the following: Mr. J. C. Fitzpatrick, Assistant Chief, Division of Manuscripts, Library of Congress; Captain Edwin T. Pollock, U. S. Navy, Superintendent, and Mr. William D. Horigan, Librarian, of the United States Naval Observatory; Captain Dudley W. Knox, U. S. Navy (Retired), Superintendent, and Miss Nannie Dornin Barney, Archivist, of the Naval Records and Library of the Navy Department; Mr. Andrew Keogh, Librarian, Yale University Library; Mr. H. M. Lydenberg, Reference Librarian, New York Public Library; Mr. Charles F. D. Belden, Director of the Public Library of the City of Boston; Miss Helen C. Bates, Reference Librarian, Detroit Public Library; Dr. William G. Stanard, Corresponding Secretary and Librarian, Virginia Historial Society; Mr. Edward V. Valentine, Acting President of the Virginia Historical Society; Dr. H. R. McIlwaine, Librarian of the Virginia State Library; R. H. Crockett, Esq., Miss Susie Gentry, and Mr. Park Marshall, Vice President of the Tennessee Historical Society,—all of Franklin, Tennessee; Mr. John

Trotwood Moore, State Librarian and Archivist, and Mr. A. P. Foster, Assistant Librarian and Archivist, Tennessee State Library, Nashville; President A. B. Chandler, Jr., State Teachers College, Fredericksburg, Virginia, and Mrs. V. M. Fleming, President of the Kenmore Association, Fredericksburg; Mr. John W. Herndon, Alexandria, Virginia; Harold T. Clark, Esq., of Squire, Sanders and Demsey, Counsellors at Law, Cleveland, Ohio; William M. Robinson, Jr., Augusta, Georgia; Mr. Gaston Lichstenstein, Corresponding Secretary of the Matthew Fontaine Maury Association, Richmond; and, last but by no means least, Assistant Professor Richard Johnson Duval, Librarian, Mr. Lewis H. Bolander, Assistant Librarian, and Mr. James M. Saunders, Cataloguer, of the United States Naval Academy Library, Annapolis, Maryland.

C. L. L.

Annapolis, Maryland.

"When I became old enough to reflect, it was the aim at which all my energies were directed to make myself a useful man. I soon found that occupation, for some useful end or other, was the true secret of happiness."

(Maury to Rutson Maury, August 31, 1840.)

"It's the talent of industry that makes a man. I don't think that so much depends upon intellect as is generally supposed; but *industry and steadiness of purpose*, they are the things."

(Maury to Frank Minor, July 25, 1855.)

CONTENTS

CONTENTS

LIST OF ILLUSTRATIONS

TENTATIVE MODEL OF THE MAURY MONUMENT

Soon to be erected in Richmond, Virginia. The monument will be 28 feet high; diameter of globe, 9 feet; height of Maury, 7 feet (1½ life size); figures of group, life size. Through the efforts of the Matthew Fontaine Maury Association a sum of over $60,000 was raised for this beautiful memorial. Sculptor F. William Sievers. See page 251.

CHAPTER I

His Early Years

No other great American has ever received so many honors abroad and so little recognition at home as has the oceanographer, Matthew Fontaine Maury. While his own country was but meagerly, and sometimes grudgingly, rewarding him, there was hardly a civilized foreign country that did not bestow upon him some mark of distinguished consideration. This was not merely a case of distance lending enchantment to the view, but rather one of perspective; those near him with but few exceptions had only a partial and incomplete view of the man, while foreigners at a distance saw the complete figure of the great scientist unobscured by the haze of professional jealousy or political and sectional prejudice. But there is another kind of perspective,—that produced by the lapse of time; hence it is that we now are enabled to appreciate the greatness of a man irrespective of the side he took in the War between the States in those "unhappy things and battles long ago". It is this perspective of time that makes possible the writing of this biography with the confidence that the time has now come when throughout our entire country Maury's greatness as a scientist and as a man will be seen in its true proportions, and his fine struggle against obstacles to attain his ideals and accomplish his purposes will serve as an inspiration and a challenge to every American.

Whatever the obstacles were that Maury had to contend with, there was no handicap in his ancestry, for

1

he was distinctively well-born. Through his father, Richard Maury, he was descended from a very distinguished Huguenot family which came to Virginia in 1718. His mother, Diana Minor, was of Dutch ancestry, being descended from Dudas Minor, who received in 1665 a grant of land in Virginia from King Charles II. The Minors intermarried with the colonial aristocracy of the Old Dominion, and there was accordingly added to the mixed Huguenot and Dutch ancestry of Matthew Fontaine Maury some of the best English blood in the colonies. Thus it was that he inherited pride of family, an inclination to scholarly pursuits, a deeply religious nature, and the character and bearing of a gentleman.

Matthew Fontaine Maury was born, the fourth son in a large family of five sons and four daughters, on January 14, 1806, on his father's farm near Fredericksburg, Virginia, and named after his paternal great-grandfathers. There had been many migrations from Spottsylvania and Albemarle counties to the free lands of the Old Southwest; and when Matthew was but five years old, his father determined to attempt to better his fortunes by following his uncle, Abram Maury, who had already established himself on the Tennessee frontier. Practically no details as to the incidents that occurred on this long and toilsome trek have been preserved; but there is a tradition in the family that all the goods and chattels were transported in wagons, and that, when little Matthew grew tired of walking or cramped from riding in the rough, jolting wagons, he was frequently carried on the back of one of his sisters. Their experiences were, no doubt, similar to those of thousands of other early pioneers who went to the Old Southwest to lay the foundations of new commonwealths.

The travel-worn family established a new home near Franklin, Tennessee, some eighteen miles north of Nashville. This section of the country was then on the outskirts of the western frontier, and it was in such an environment that young Maury spent the most formative years of his life. As a lad, he had to take his share of the burdensome work on the farm; and it appears from an incident long afterwards related by his brother that he had the distaste for farm work, which is common to boys. Their father had set them to work picking cotton, and Matthew showed his inventiveness by devising a way of shortening their labor. He suggested to his brother that they make short work of the cotton picking by pulling off the cotton balls bodily and cramming them into an old hollow hickory stump that was full of water. The scheme was a good one so long as it was undiscovered, but after a time the watchful eye of their father detected the boys in the act and a flogging was the result. The lives of the children on the frontier, however, were by no means wholly filled with toil. There was ample opportunity to enjoy outdoor sports in all seasons of the year, and indoors the Maury family were not without resources for passing the time pleasantly and profitably. There were traditions of culture and even of scholarship in the family, and besides it should be remembered that the homes of the early settlers were rarely without at least a few good books.

Maury's father, having observed that his own father had been too stern with his children, treated his large family with considerable indulgence; yet he was strict as to their religious training in the home and gathered the children together morning and night each day to read the Psalter antiphonally. In this way Matthew became so familiar with the Psalms of David that years afterwards he could give a quotation and cite chapter and verse as though he had the Bible before him. This early religious influence later colored all Maury's thinking and writing to a very marked degree. His mother, who was known as a woman of great decision of character, endowed her son with this same quality which is so essential to greatness; while her husband passed on to Matthew much of his amiability and ingenuousness for which he was greatly liked throughout the neighborhood.

Maury received his elementary education in an "Old Field" school, where the seats were made of split logs with peg legs, where there were no blackboards and but few books, and where the pupils studied their lessons aloud. This method of study probably led to the custom of "singing geography", the pupils being ranged round the room to chant geographical facts. Whether Maury was thus inducted into the mysteries of that science which his researches were afterwards so greatly to enrich is not known, for the only schoolbook that he makes reference to in his letters is the famous Webster's "Blueback Speller", which he says was the first book that was ever placed in his hands.

A better education than that afforded in these country elementary schools was, however, destined for Maury. When he was in his twelfth year, a dangerous fall from a tree so injured his back as to cause his father to consider it unwise for the lad to continue to work on the farm. He had already shown such aptitude for study that it was decided to send him to Harpeth Academy, then located about two miles from Franklin. In this school, Maury had as teachers the Reverend Doctor Blackburn, afterwards Chaplain to Congress; James Otey, who became the first Bishop of Tennessee; and William C. Hasbrouck, who was afterwards a distinguished lawyer in his native state, New York. The impression that Maury made upon these scholarly men was a very favorable and lasting one, and he retained their warm personal friendship as long as they lived.

It was with Dr. Blackburn that Maury began the study of Latin grammar, through which he marched with seven league boots in only seven days; this, of course, was a record for the school. Though he thus showed a capacity for learning languages, both at this time and later in the navy while on foreign stations, yet the field of science held the greatest attraction for Maury. His ambition to become a mathematician was aroused in a curious way. "The first man of science I ever saw in my infant days in the West", he said, "was a shoemaker —old Mr. Neil. He was a mathematician; he worked out his problems with his awl on leather, and would send home his shoes with their soles covered with little x's and y's. The example of that man first awakened in my breast the young spirit of emulation; for my earliest recollections of the feelings of ambition are connected with the aspiration to emulate that man in mathematics". The ambition to know and achieve early displayed itself in Maury, and in later life he pleasantly recalled to mind his "Tennessee school days when the air was filled with castles".

Such, in brief, was the life of Maury as a lad in his adopted state,—a state which he came to love and to which he referred years afterwards, when he had traveled extensively and become a famous man, as "the loveliest of lands" and "the finest country I have ever seen". Here he was nurtured with the best the frontier life had to offer, and given independence of mind, courage, and self-reliance; love of honor and a chivalrous respect for woman; an unassuming modesty which bordered on diffidence and bashfulness; a strongly religious inclination; and a burning desire to know and to achieve. With this equipment he would doubtless have made a name for himself if he had remained in Tennessee; but Providence directed his steps into a broader field where he was able to gain for himself much greater distinction,—one that was not alone national but international in its scope.

One of the well marked characteristics of Maury's maturity was the breadth of his intellectual vision. His mind loved to exercise itself with large problems, and questions of world-wide interest. This trait in his character could not have been developed so well perhaps in any other career as in the one he chose,—service in the navy of the United States. In this connection, it is interesting to note that Maury's father wished him to study medicine and promised him financial assistance in such an undertaking. As a physician, he doubtless would have reached great eminence and the science of medicine would almost certainly have received contributions from his original mind; but a military career presented greater attractions for the lad. At one time he considered entering West Point as a cadet, but some one returned from there with an unfavorable report and, besides, the bare mention of such a plan put his father in a rage; hence he decided against the army and instead determined to enter the United States Navy.

There were very good reasons for Maury's wishing to become a naval officer. Indeed, all his life he had had a close personal interest in that branch of the government service. His eldest brother, John Minor Maury, at the age of thirteen, even before the family had left Virginia, had become a midshipman. He then had thrilling adventures in the South Seas, was with David Porter in the *Essex* during the bloody battle with the English at Valparaiso, and afterwards fought with Macdonough in the Battle of Lake Champlain. All this was enough to awaken the spirit of adventure and arouse the desire of emulation in the heart of a younger brother. And though John Maury had the misfortune, in 1824, to die of yellow fever on board his ship and be buried at sea off Norfolk, yet Matthew clung firmly to his decision in the face of the opposition of his family, particularly his father, to the entrance of a second son into so hazardous a profession.

Maury secured his midshipman's warrant with comparative ease, through General Sam Houston, who was at that time the Representative of that district in Congress. This appointment was gotten, however, without his parents' knowledge, and when it became known to his father he expressed his disapproval of his son's conduct in very strong terms and determined to leave him to his own resources. But young Maury was very resourceful and contrived to purchase for seventy-five dollars a gray mare from his cousin Abram Maury's overseer, which he was to sell upon reaching his destination, and then he was to repay the money. Still he had practically nothing for traveling expenses, but this obstacle was removed by his teacher, Mr. Hasbrouck, who gave him thirty dollars for assistance he had rendered in teaching the younger pupils in the Academy.

On the day of his departure on that Sunday in the spring of 1825, Maury's father refused to tell him goodbye and turned his back,—it is said, not so much in anger as in sorrow at his leaving home.   No doubt the lad's heart was saddened by this circumstance as well as by the parting from the rest of the family, especially from his favorite brother Richard, only two years his senior, who had always been his inseparable companion.   But he put on a brave front, mounted his "snow white steed", and set forth on the long lonesome ride to Virginia, whence he was to make his way to Washington and there embark on his new career.

The second or third day from home at an inn in East Tennessee, the young traveler fell in with two merchants, Read and Echols, from Huntsville, Alabama, on their way to Baltimore to purchase goods, and in company with these gentlemen he traveled as far as Fincastle, Virginia.   Though he greatly enjoyed their company, he was much concerned lest they find out his financial condition, suspect his poverty, and humiliate him by offering him money.   His resources were indeed sadly depleted on crossing over into Virginia, where his money had to be exchanged for coin of that state at a ruinous discount of twenty per cent, and when, after a journey of two weeks, he reached the home of his Cousin Reuben Maury near Charlottesville, he had but fifty cents left.

Here a special entertainment was given in his honor, and Maury had his first experience with the society manners of the East which were somewhat more refined than those of the Tennessee frontier.   When the negro servant passed him a saucer of ice-cream and a spoon, he very modestly placed only a spoonful in his plate and left the remainder to be passed to the others, thinking that it was some kind of strange sauce.   From this place he proceeded to the home of his Uncle Edward Herndon,

From De Meissner's "Old Naval Days," through courtesy of Henry Holt and Company.

U.S.S. "BRANDYWINE," COMMANDER BIDDLE, OFF MALTA, NOVEMBER 6, 1831; AND U. S. S. "CONCORD," CAPTAIN PERRY, IN BACKGROUND

near Fredericksburg; and while visiting there, he met the young girl who was some years afterwards to become his wife. She was Ann Hull Herndon, the eldest daughter of Dabney Herndon, who was a banker and prominent citizen of Fredericksburg. It was a case of love at first sight with young Maury, who was completely captivated by the blue eyes, auburn hair, and musical voice of his fair cousin; while she in turn was very favorably impressed with this relative from the West with his ruddy complexion which she used to say after they were married reminded her of "David fresh from his sheep with his sling".

When he arrived at his destination in Washington, the Secretary of the Navy allowed him fifteen cents a mile as mileage from Franklin, Tennessee, and this fairly put Maury's head above water financially. After a short visit with relatives here, he went on to New York where he had been ordered to report on board the U. S. Frigate *Brandywine.*

Here he arrived August 13, 1825, and at once entered into active service in the profession which he had chosen. He has left no record as to what his thoughts and feelings were during those weeks when he, a lad from the West who had never seen a ship before, was adjusting himself to those new and strange surroundings. But that he had made up his mind to succeed in his chosen career, whether he liked it or not, is evident from this sentiment which occurs more than once in his letters: " . . . to the old rule with which I set out on horseback from Tennessee in 1825, a fresh midshipman, 'Make everything bend to your profession' ".

CHAPTER II

His Three Cruises

Maury's early years in the navy afforded the lad from the backwoods of Tennessee wonderful experiences, and excellent opportunities for supplementing the desultory education that he had received. To a young man of his intellectual capacity, these voyages to foreign lands during the most plastic years of his life were invaluable in the development of a mind capable of grappling later with questions and problems which concerned the entire world.

Luckily for the young officer, the very first ship to which he was attached, the *Brandywine*, was the vessel which had been chosen to convey Lafayette home to France after his memorable visit to the United States. This ship, named from Brandywine Creek, the scene of the battle in which Lafayette was wounded on September 11, 1777, had been launched on June 16 of the year 1825. In equipping her for this special service, the officers had been selected so as to represent as many different states as possible and, where it was practicable, they were to be descendants of persons who had distinguished themselves in the Revolution. This accounted for the large number of midshipmen ordered aboard her, twenty-six instead of the usual eight or ten for a vessel of that size. Maury was thus brought in touch with young officers from various sections of the country; and among the senior officers were Captain Charles Morris, who had made a name for himself in the War of 1812, and Lieutenant David Farragut, who was to become one of the very greatest American naval leaders.

On the 8th of September the *Brandywine* set sail from the mouth of the Potomac, where Lafayette had been received on board the ship. She passed down the Chesapeake through a brilliant rainbow which was apparently supported on the Virginia and Maryland shores, as if Nature had reserved to herself the honor of erecting the last of the numerous triumphal arches that had been dedicated to the great Frenchman during his extraordinary visit. As the ship made her way to sea, almost the last glimpse which Lafayette had of America was the bluffs of the York River where he had so materially aided the American cause at the Battle of Yorktown.

The voyage turned out to be not a very pleasant one, for the ship had hardly gotten under way when she began to leak and for a time it was thought that she would have to return to port. But as it was reported that the leak was under control, Lafayette advised the captain to continue the voyage, and when the planks of the vessel swelled from immersion in the water the leak gradually diminished. The weather, however, then became stormy, and during most of the passage the distinguished passenger suffered so severely from sea-sickness and gout that he was unable to join the officers at dinner or to visit the deck. They were thus deprived, much to their regret, from listening as much as they desired to the reminiscences of the great general's interesting and eventful life. There was another unpleasantness that affected the midshipmen in particular. This was caused by a steward who, in cleaning an officer's uniform, upset a bottle of turpentine, the contents of which ran into a barrel of sugar belonging to the midshipmen's mess.

As a consequence, during the remainder of the voyage they had to eat their desserts strongly flavored with turpentine.

At the close of the voyage, the midshipmen presented to Lafayette, as a mark of their personal friendship, a beautiful silver urn appropriately engraved with scenes of the Capitol at Washington, Lafayette's visit to the tomb of Washington, and the arrival of the *Brandywine* at Havre. At this French port, Lafayette disembarked, taking with him the flag of the American vessel as a souvenir of the voyage. From here Maury's ship proceeded to Cowes where she was calked, and then sailed for the Mediterranean, joining Commodore John Rodgers' squadron at Gibraltar on the 2nd of November. The ship was refitted here during the winter, and the following spring she returned to the United States, arriving at New York in May, 1826.

Such in brief outline was Maury's first cruise. Though none of his letters giving his impressions of these first months at sea have been preserved, yet it is not difficult to imagine with what eagerness and delight his active young mind observed the strange sights and assimilated the new experiences. Many years afterwards he wrote of how he secured a Spanish work on navigation in order that he might acquire a new language and a science at the same time. In this connection he related how he resorted to various artifices for study while on watch. "If I went below only for a moment or two," he wrote, "and could lay hands upon a dictionary or any book, I would note a sentence, or even a word, that I did not understand, and fix it in my memory to be reflected upon when I went on deck. I used to draw problems in spherical trigonometry with chalk on the shot, and put them in the racks where I could see them as I walked the deck. That with so much perseverance I should have failed in my prime object, I attribute to the want of books and proper teachers in the navy". It was this seriousness of purpose and industry that caused Maury soon to become well known among his shipmates for his scholarship, and the story is told that even on this first cruise a certain mathematical problem was passed from steerage to wardroom without solution until he solved it.

After making a short visit to his home in Tennessee, Maury set sail on June 10, 1826 from Norfolk on the frigate *Macedonian* to which he had been ordered for temporary duty. This ship was bound for Rio Janeiro where she arrived after a passage of sixty-two days. After cruising in Brazilian waters for awhile, the frigate went on down the coast to Montevideo. At this time a war was raging between Brazil and Argentina over Banda Oriental, or Uruguay, which had been a sort of political football between the two countries until 1821, when it was partly subdued by Brazil. In 1825, however, it rose against this empire, and after a long struggle of three years it succeeded in having its independence recognized by the treaty of Rio Janeiro, on August 27, 1828. This state of affairs constituted the principal reason why American ships of war were sent to those waters. Thus was Maury brought into touch with history in the making, and the letters which he wrote at this time show an alert interest in what he was observing and display as well an unusual ability in recording experiences and his impressions of the people.

His name was still carried on the muster and pay rolls of the *Brandywine*; but that ship did not depart for

South American waters until the last of August, 1826, when she set sail from New York with the *Vincennes*. Eventually it was Maury's good fortune to be transferred to the latter vessel, in which he was to circumnavigate the globe. He first joined the *Vincennes*, on March 10, 1827, in Callao Roads, the port of Lima, Peru. The American warships had by this time entered the Pacific and were cruising up and down the South American coast from Valparaiso, Chile to Guayaquil, Ecuador to protect the commerce of the United States, as this part of South America also was then in turmoil.

Bolivar, after liberating the states of northern South America from Spanish rule, was endeavoring to organize Columbia, Peru, Bolivia, La Plata, and Chile into a grand republic, of which he aspired to be the ruler. The union of the first three of these states was practically realized, but the undertaking finally ended in failure because of the jealousy of Bolivar's former companions in arms and the fickleness of the South American people. This characteristic of the people is humorously set forth in Maury's letters in which he describes some of the fighting which he witnessed at Guayaquil. The young man's historical outlook was thus further broadened by this personal contact with the affairs of the great *Libertador*, Bolivar.

On July 4, 1829, the war meanwhile having come to an end, the *Vincennes*, under the command of Captain William Compton (Bolton) Finch, set forth from Callao on her voyage across the Pacific. She was to make her first stop at the Washington Islands, now known as the Marquesas, in order, as Captain Finch's orders read, to secure proper treatment from the natives for any of our defenseless seafaring countrymen who in their lawful pursuits were compelled by necessity to resort to the harbors of the islands for refreshment and supplies; to reclaim those who from improper motives had remained among the islanders; and by exhibiting the moral advancement of America to so raise the American national character in their estimation as to induce a praiseworthy imitation of it on their part. The ship arrived at one of the islands, Nukahiva by name, on July 26, and in order to carry out the spirit of his orders Captain Finch made his vessel a "tabu ship" that he might prevent the gross licentiousness to which ships from Christian lands were usually surrendered in those ports.

For an account of Maury's experiences on this cruise little is to be derived from his extant letters, but fortunately Chaplain C. S. Stewart wrote a book entitled "A Visit to the South Seas in the U. S. Ship Vincennes during the years 1829 and 1830", in which he mentions Maury as a member of the shore party which visited the Valley of Taioa and as one of those who went on various other expeditions on the island of Nukahiva under the direction of the chaplain. That these were unforgettable experiences is evident from Stewart's rapturous descriptions of the people and the scenery of the island which, he declared, "seemed almost a fairy land, scarce less fascinating in its features than the imaginary haunts pictured by the pens of genius as the abode of Calypso, or the happy valley of the Abyssinian prince".

Before leaving this island Maury had an experience of peculiar interest. It was here that his brother John had spent two years practically cut off from civilization. Just before the War of 1812, he had secured a furlough from the navy and had gone as first officer in a merchantman on a voyage to China. On departing from Nukahiva, the captain of this ship left John Maury and six men on the island to procure sandalwood and other articles of commerce. They were, of course, to be taken off on the return from China; but the war broke out and the ship was blockaded in a Chinese port by the English. Meanwhile the Americans were left to shift for themselves on Nukahiva, and in a war between two tribes, one of which was friendly to them, all the white men were killed except John Maury and another man named Baker. Fortunately, Porter visited the island during the famous cruise of the *Essex*, and rescued the two survivors. In order that he might learn something about the history of his brother while on the island, Midshipman Maury set about studying the language of the natives, during the three weeks or so of his visit. And shortly before his departure he was able to converse with the old chief who had been his brother's friend. "The Happas and the Typees", Maury wrote, "were at war. The latter having just captured three children from the former, we went to the rescue and recovered two, the third had been eaten. When we returned to the Happa Valley from the expedition—it was the valley where dwelt my brother—the men had liberty and the old Happa chief remained on board as a hostage, for his subjects were all a set of savages and the women literally in the fig leaf state. At night when all the men had come off safe and sound, and a few days only before we left, I was sent to take the old fellow ashore. Going ashore, I made myself known to him. He was the firm and fast friend of my brother. Had saved his life. He was then old. He it was that offered me his scepter, his own wife, and the daughter of a neighboring chief if I would remain".

Needless to say, this flattering offer was rejected, and

Maury was on the *Vincennes* when she sailed away from the island. In leaving the bay, the ship narrowly escaped destruction, for the vessel was at first becalmed and then suddenly carried by the swell toward the breakers. Every face was pale with fear and the silence of the grave hung over the ship, but a timely breath of air filled the topsails and finally slowly carried her out to the open sea. In five days she was seven hundred miles away at Tahiti, one of the Society Islands. Here Maury had the pleasure of joining several shore parties, and was also present at an interesting reception to the Queen of Tahiti on board the *Vincennes*, when the firing of the salute to the queen greatly alarmed her and caused her to behave in a very humorous and undignified manner.

The ship then set sail, after a month's visit, for the Sandwich Islands. On the island of Hawaii Maury visited the Cascade of the Rainbow and probably saw also the volcano of Kilauea, about both of which Chaplain Stewart goes into rhapsodies in his account of the voyage. Captain Finch went also to Honolulu, on the island of Oahu, and there presented to King Kamehameha III a pair of gloves and a large map of the United States, and a silver vase to the regent and two silver goblets to the princess. A letter from the Secretary of the Navy was then delivered to the king. This was well received by his majesty, and his reply was in the friendliest possible tone, agreeing to treat American sailors with more consideration and fairness in the future. The purpose of the visit having thus been accomplished, several deserters having been reclaimed, and the settlement of claims for about $50,000 for American citizens having been negotiated, the ship departed for China.

Leaving behind the northern Bashee Islands, which are considered one of the barriers of the Pacific as well as one of the portals to the Celestial Empire, the ship came to anchor on January 3, 1830 in the roads of Macao, a Portuguese city, situated on a small island about seventy miles from Canton. The *Vincennes* thus gained the distinction of being the second American man-of-war to visit Chinese waters, having been preceded only by the *Congress* in 1819. After receiving a statement from the American consul and merchants at Canton on the advisability of having American men-of-war make periodic visits to Chinese waters, Captain Finch was off again, this time for the Philippines.

After a brief visit at Manila, the ship turned towards home, and, stopping in the Straits of Sunda and at Cape Town, on the first of May came in sight of the Island of St. Helena. Here ample time was afforded the officers for seeing Longwood House in which Napoleon had lived and also his tomb, from which the body of the great general had not at that time been removed to Paris. After leaving this island, the ship made no other stop until she arrived in New York on the 8th of June, 1830, with her band appropriately playing, "Hail Columbia! Happy Land!"

After almost four years to a day, Maury was home again; but he was no longer the raw lad from the Tennessee backwoods, for the information and experience which he had gained on this cruise of the first American man-of-war to circumnavigate the globe had gone a long way towards taking the place of a college education. Men of the stamp of Commodore Charles Morris, Lieutenant Farragut, Captain Finch, Chaplain Stewart, and dozens of other officers with whom he had come in contact during his first two cruises had contributed, by example at least, in making him into an officer and a gentleman. During all this time he had studied, and read as widely as opportunity afforded, having had the privilege for a portion of the time of using the books of Midshipman William Irving, a nephew to Washington Irving.

That the opportunities for instruction on shipboard were, however, very limited is indicated by the following summary of Maury's experience with the school system of the navy. "The first ship I sailed in", he wrote, "had a schoolmaster: a young man from Connecticut. He was well qualified and well disposed to teach navigation, but not having a schoolroom, or authority to assemble the midshipmen, the cruise passed off without the opportunity of organizing his school. From him, therefore, we learned nothing. On my next cruise, the dominie was a Spaniard; and, being bound to South America, there was a perfect mania in the steerage for the Spanish language. In our youthful impetuosity we bought books, and for a week or so pursued the study with great eagerness. But our spirits began to flag, and the difficulties of *ser* and *estar* finally laid the copestone for us over the dominie's vernacular. The study was exceedingly dry. We therefore voted both teacher and grammar a bore, and committing the latter to the deep, with one accord, we declared in favor of the Byronical method—

> ' 'Tis pleasant to be taught in a strange tongue
>   By female lips and eyes';

and continued to defer our studies till we should arrive in the South American vale of paradise, called Valparaiso. After arriving on that station, the commander, who had often expressed his wish that we should learn to speak Spanish, sent down 'for all the young gentlemen', as the middies are called, and commenced to ask us one by one—'Can you speak Spanish?' 'No, sir.' 'Then you are no gentleman'. 'Can you?' But always receiving the same answer, he sent us out of the cabin as a set of blackguards. As he was as ignorant on this subject as any of us, we included him among the number, and thought it an excellent joke. Thus ended our scholastic duties on that ship. I was afterwards transferred to another vessel in which the schoolmaster was a young lawyer, who knew more about *jetsam* and *flotsam* than about lunars and dead reckoning—at least, I presume so, for he never afforded us an opportunity to judge of his knowledge on the latter subjects. He was not on speaking terms with the reefers, ate up all the plums for the duff, and was finally turned out of the ship as a nuisance. When I went to sea again, the teacher was an amiable and accomplished young man, from the 'land of schoolmasters and leather pumpkin seed'. Poor fellow!—far gone in consumption, had a field of usefulness been open to him, he could not have labored in it. He went to sea for his health, but never returned. There was no schoolmaster in the next ship, and the 'young gentlemen' were as expert at lunars, and as *au fait* in the mysteries of latitude and departure, as any I had seen. In my next ship, the dominie was a young man, troubled like some of your correspondents, Mr. Editor, with *cacoethes scribendi*. He wrote a book. But I never saw him teaching 'the young idea', or instructing the young gentlemen in the art of plain sailing; nor did I think it was his fault, for he had neither schoolroom nor pupil. Such is my experience of the school system in the navy; and I believe that of every officer will tally with it".[1]

Maury had the privilege of continuing his studies ashore in New York and Washington for several months before he embarked on his next cruise. He was then preparing himself for the examination for the rank of passed midshipman. This examination covered the following subjects: Bowditch's "Navigation"; Playfair's "Euclid", Books 1, 2, 3, 4, and 6; McClure's "Spherics"; Spanish or French; Mental and Moral Philosophy; Bourdon's "Algebra"; and Seamanship. The time devoted to each midshipman by the examiners, in the order of his appointment, ranged from fifty minutes to two hours. To judge from the questions in seamanship, the examination was largely of a very practical nature,—on how to handle the sails of a ship and how to navigate her.

In his examination, Maury passed twenty-seven in a class of forty. An explanation of this apparently low standing may be gathered from the following account of the manner of conducting such examinations: "The midshipman who seeks to become learned in the branches of science that pertain to his profession, and who before the Examining Board should so far stray from the lids of Bowditch as to get among the isodynamic and other lines of a magnetic chart, would be blackballed as certainly as though he were to clubhaul a ship for the Board in the Hebrew tongue. . . . Midshipmen, turning to Bowditch, commit to memory the formula of his first or second method for 'finding the longitude at sea by a lunar observation'. Thus crammed or 'drilled', as it is called, they go before the Board of Examination, where, strange to say, there is a premium offered for such quali-

[1] "Scraps from a Lucky Bag" in *Southern Literary Messenger*, May, 1840.

fication. He who repeats 'by heart' the rules of Bow-ditch, though he does not understand the mathematical principles involved in one of them, obtains a higher number from the Board than he who, skilled in mathematics, goes to the blackboard and, drawing his diagram, can demonstrate every problem in navigation".[2] Maury, no doubt, wrote this out of his own personal experience; and even though the results of his examination may have indicated that in the ordinary duties of his profession he was not above the average, still it was to be in a special field of the service that his genius was to display itself.

During the winter which Maury spent in Washington he fell completely in love with his cousin, Ann Herndon, who was visiting relatives in Georgetown. Hitherto there had been a certain safety in numbers, as indicated by the numerous references in his letters to the charms of English girls and the "piercing eyes and insinuating smiles" of the Brazilian and Peruvian maidens. But before he went to sea again he became engaged to his cousin, and on his departure he gave her a little seal which was to be used only when she wrote to him; it bore the inscription of the single word *Mizpah*, that beautiful Biblical parting salutation, "The Lord watch between thee and me when we are absent one from the other".

This love affair caused Maury to consider resigning from the naval service, but his hope of getting employment as a surveyor did not materialize and he finally concluded that he supposed Uncle Sam would have the selling of his bones to the doctors. Accordingly, in June, 1831 he sailed again for the Pacific, this time in the *Falmouth*. His ship touched at Rio for a brief visit,

[2] *Ibid.*, December, 1840.

then doubled Cape Horn, and arrived at Valparaiso the last of October. The *Falmouth* remained on this station for about a year, and Maury renewed his former acquaintances and enjoyed the hospitality of Chilean society at dances and dinners without number. The vessel then cruised further north along the coast, visiting various ports and remaining several months at Callao.

One of Maury's shipmates on this cruise has left some reminiscences which throw considerable light upon his young friend's qualities as an officer. "I encountered some ridicule", wrote Captain Whiting, "from my messmates for predicting that Maury would be a distinguished man. I asserted that there was that in him which could not be kept down. . . . In a survey of San Lorenzo Island while attached to the *Falmouth* I was an assistant to Maury, and he displayed that perseverance and energy undismayed by difficulty when he had once determined upon accomplishing a result, which ever marked his career. In prosecuting the survey of the Boca del Diables he scaled rocks and crept around the corners of cliffs when I was almost afraid to follow him, but the attainment of his object seemed to be with him the only subject of his thoughts. He landed on the Labos Rocks to the westward of San Lorenzo to make some astronomical and trigonometrical observations while I remained in the boat. When he landed it was almost a dead calm, and the sea comparatively smooth; but by the time he had finished his observations a fresh wind had sprung up from the southwards, the tide had risen, and the sea was raging so as to forbid the near approach of the boat, one minute receding from the rock so as to leave a yawning gulf of twenty or thirty feet depth, then rushing up again with appalling and irresistible force. Calling on me to approach as near as I dared, Maury ascended to the highest point of the rock, took off his jacket, and with a string which he found in his pocket tied in it his watch and sextant, and then threw it with all his might into the sea toward the boat, while the bowman of the boat stood ready to seize it with his boathook before the water had time to penetrate the wrapping. Maury then, watching the culmination of a wave, sprang from the rock himself and being a good swimmer and possessed of much youthful strength reached the boat in safety, but it was a fearful leap".

The seeds of Maury's later wonderful achievements in the science of the sea were implanted during this cruise of the *Falmouth*. He was the sailing master of the ship, and naturally wished to make as quick a voyage as possible. Before sailing he had searched diligently for information concerning the winds and currents and the best course for his ship to take, and was astonished to find that there was practically no information on the subject to be secured. The observations of these phenomena of the sea which he accordingly made on this voyage turned his mind toward a series of investigations which later was to make his name known round the entire world.

Maury did not return to the United States in the *Falmouth*, but shortly before her departure from Callao he was transferred on August 20, 1833 to the schooner *Dolphin*, in which vessel he performed the duties of first lieutenant. He remained on the little schooner but a few weeks, and then was attached to the frigate *Potomac*, which had just arrived at Callao under the command of Captain John Downes. This ship had been on duty on the Pacific coast of South America for a little more than a year, after having cruised almost around the world by way of the Cape of Good Hope, the Malay Archipelago, China, and the South Seas.

In a short time, however, the *Potomac* sailed for home, arriving at Valparaiso the middle of December. Here, according to Captain Whiting, Maury had a very unpleasant experience with a young lady named Manuela Poma with whom he had previously become acquainted. Her hand had been sought by a young officer of the Chilean army, who the evening before the *Potomac* sailed came on board the ship and told Maury that he had destroyed all his hopes of happiness. He said that the previous day he had made a declaration of his love to Manuela and that she had rejected him, telling him that her affections were already bestowed on the young American naval officer. Instead of priding himself on this conquest, as many young men would have done, Maury was exceedingly distressed as he had considered his relationship with the young girl to have been nothing more than that of friendship, and by a returning ship he sent a long letter to Manuela. Soon after his arrival in Boston he learned that she had died of consumption.

The voyage home round the Horn and by way of Rio was more or less uneventful, except for imminent peril for a time from icebergs off the Falkland Islands. After three years Maury was home again, and according to the decrees of Fate this was to be his last cruise. Hence a distinctive period in his life had come to a close; but his nine years of almost continuous sea duty had been a splendid preparation for the peculiar scientific work that he was soon to undertake.

CHAPTER III

He Resorts to the Pen

When the *Potomac* arrived in Boston, Maury applied for leave of absence and went directly to Fredericksburg, Virginia, where he was married to Ann Herndon on July 15, 1834. In this charming old Virginia town he established his residence for the next seven years, living on Charlotte Street in a two-story frame house with a large old-fashioned garden, which he rented from a Mr. Johnston. He had always been generous with his money to different members of his family, and it is related that, as a consequence, he had but twenty dollars of ready money at the time of his marriage, all of which he gave as a fee to Parson E. C. McGuire. In the same generous way he shared his home for a considerable time with his brother John's widow and her two sons.

With some leisure at his command, Maury determined to become an author, under the encouragement of the recent appearance in the *American Journal of Science and Arts* of his first scientific article, "On the Navigation of Cape Horn". This, the first fruit of his sea experience, described forcefully the dangers of the passage of Cape Horn, and gave specific information concerning the winds and the peculiar rising and falling of the barometer in those latitudes. In the same number of this journal there appeared another article describing Maury's "Plan of an Instrument for Finding the True Lunar Distance", the instrument in question having been invented by him. With these beginnings, he ambitiously set to work to finish a book on navigation, which he had commenced

Courtesy of "The Journal of American History," Vol. IV, Number 3 (1910).

LIEUT. M. F. MAURY

From a daguerreotype of about the year 1855

during the last part of his recent tour of sea duty. He did not expect to receive much direct profit from such a nautical book, but hoped that it might be of a collateral advantage to him in making his name known to the Navy Department and to his brother officers. As it was the first nautical work of science ever to come from the pen of an American naval officer, he expected to base a claim for promotion on the merits of the book, and had hopes of being made a lieutenant of ten years' rank with the accompanying back pay amounting to $4,000 or $5,000.

These plans of Maury's did not fully materialize. President Jackson was of the opinion that the young author deserved promotion for his scientific work and reimbursement for the money which he had expended in its publication, but the Secretary of the Navy, Mahlon Dickerson, did not carry out the President's wishes. The book itself, however, was a great success on its appearance early in the year 1836, under the title of "A New Theoretical and Practical Treatise on Navigation". The publishers, E. C. and J. Biddle of Philadelphia, soon had the pleasure of printing a long list of favorable opinions of the work from professors and distinguished officers in the navy, among which the commendation of Nathaniel Bowditch gave Maury the greatest satisfaction. His book very quickly took the place of Bowditch's "Practical Navigator" as a textbook for junior officers in the navy, and when the Naval Academy was established at Annapolis it was used for several years as the basis of the instruction given to midshipmen in navigation. In the title page appeared the significant words, "Cur Non?" (Why not?), the motto adopted by Lafayette when he espoused the cause of the American colonies; this was in effect Maury's answer to any query that might be made as to why a young naval officer should attempt the writing of a book.

Of the reviews of Maury's work, one of the most interesting appeared in the *Southern Literary Messenger* of June, 1836. It was written by Edgar Allan Poe, who was then editor of that magazine, and closed with the following paragraph: "The spirit of literary improvement has been awakened among the officers of our gallant navy. We are pleased to see that science also is gaining votaries from its ranks. Hitherto how little have they improved the golden opportunities of knowledge which their distant voyages held forth, and how little have they enjoyed the rich banquet which nature spreads for them in every clime they visit! But the time is coming when, imbued with a taste for science and a spirit of research, they will become ardent explorers of the regions in which they sojourn. Freighted with the knowledge which observation only can impart, and enriched with collections of objects precious to the student of nature, their return after the perils of a distant voyage will then be doubly joyful. The enthusiast in science will anxiously await their coming, and add his cordial welcome to the warm greetings of relatives and friends". Poe, perhaps, had no idea how soon his prophetic words were to be fulfilled,—and by the very man whose book he had so favorably reviewed.

After making this successful entry into the field of authorship, Maury lectured on scientific subjects in Fredericksburg and set about the studying of mineralogy, geology, and drawing. In these studies he made such progress as to qualify himself to become superintendent of the United States Gold Mine near Fredericksburg. He spent the summer of 1836 with his family at this mine where he made some important improvements in its administration.   Meanwhile, he had been promoted on June 10, 1836 to the rank of lieutenant, and though he had been offered a salary of $1200 as a mining engineer he decided to remain in the navy.

Maury's interests were next directed to the Exploring Expedition to the South Seas.   The little squadron selected to make the cruise, composed of the frigate *Macedonian* and the brigs *Pioneer* and *Consort*, rendezvoused at Norfolk in the autumn of the year 1836, under the command of Captain Thomas Ap Catesby Jones. Maury made an attempt to secure the command of one of the smaller vessels; but he failed in this, and had to be content with being attached to the *Macedonian*, March 18, 1837.   Secretary of the Navy Dickerson had not, from its inception, been in favor of the expedition, which he looked upon as a scheme by President Jackson for self-glorification.   He therefore did all that he could to block the sailing of the squadron by causing unnecessary delays, not caring for the waste of money involved in this procrastination.   In this way the ships were kept at Norfolk until October when they finally sailed for New York.

In September, Maury had had the good fortune to be appointed "Astronomer" for the expedition with $1000 additional pay, and also as assistant to the "Hydrographer", Lieutenant James Glynn.   To prepare himself for these duties he went to Philadelphia, where in a little observatory in Rittenhouse Square he soon familiarized himself with the use of astronomical instruments.   The expedition, however, still delayed to set sail, and the vexatious interference with his command so affected Captain Jones's health as to give the Secretary of the

Navy an excuse for removing him from his position. Matters had by this time come to such a pass that several officers declined the command when it was offered them; namely, Captains Shubrick, Kearny, Perry, and Gregory. Finally, in April, 1838, a junior officer, Lieutenant Charles Wilkes, though there were eighty lieutenants above his grade, was selected, and he accepted the appointment.

The sloops of war *Vincennes* and *Peacock* and two smaller vessels were chosen instead of those originally prepared, and it became necessary to reorganize the personnel of the expedition. Maury had sympathized with Captain Jones in the unjust treatment which he had received from the Secretary of the Navy, and besides he had written that Wilkes was the only officer in the navy with whom he would not coöperate provided that he was put in command of the enterprise. He therefore asked to be detached from the expedition.

Maury might possibly have had the honor of commanding the exploring expedition himself, as clearly indicated by the following letter which he wrote years afterwards: "The expedition had been taken away from the Secretary of the Navy and transferred to Poinsett, Secretary of War. I was ordered to fetch the instruments to Washington and report myself to Poinsett. He received me with open arms, took me into his bosom, and asked me to give him the names of the officers *without regard to rank* that *I* thought best qualified for the expedition. I afterwards had reason to suppose that he expected me to name myself and intended to put me in command of it, as really I was the most important personage in it—Hydrographer and Astronomer. But I asked myself, what right have I to draw distinctions among brother officers? So I gave him a list of the officers belonging to the expedition; myself, the youngest lieutenant in the navy, at the bottom of the list. He froze up with disgust, ordered Wilkes home, and gave him the command, and so I was the gainer, for I preserved mine integrity".

Maury was next assigned to the duty of surveying Southern harbors, relative to the establishment of a navy yard in the South. In this work he assisted Lieutenant James Glynn, in the schooner *Experiment* and the steamboat *Engineer*, in the examination and survey of the harbors of Beaufort and Wilmington, and the inlets Sapelo and Doboy on the coast of Georgia. Early in the month of August, 1839, Maury was detached from the *Engineer* at Norfolk with leave for one month, and he set out very soon thereafter from his home in Fredericksburg to visit his parents in Tennessee to look after some business affairs for his father who had become old and infirm, and also to make arrangements for conveying them to Virginia where they were to make their home with him.

Maury had written in vain, in February and again in August, 1839, to F. R. Hassler of the United States Coast Survey offering his services as head of a triangulation party. This was one of the several attempts he made at different times to find work of such a nature as to justify his resignation from the navy. By such small threads often hangs a man's destiny. If Hassler had accepted Maury's services, his whole future would probably have been different from what it became, for an event was soon to happen to him which, though apparently at first most unfortunate, was indirectly to place him on that flood tide which led him on to fortune.

Under orders to join the brig *Consort* at New York and continue the surveying of Southern harbors, Maury left his father's home in Tennessee by stage coach to join his ship. He went by the northern route, and near Somerset, Ohio, on a rainy night about one o'clock in the morning, an embankment gave way and the coach was upset. Maury, having given his seat inside to a woman with a baby in arms, was riding on the seat with the coachman, and was the only person seriously injured. There were twelve other passengers; Maury, the thirteenth, had his right knee-joint transversely dislocated and the thigh-bone longitudinally fractured.

His recovery from the injury was slow and painful. The leg was improperly set, and at a time when the use of anesthetics was unknown it had to be reset with great pain to the unfortunate officer. During the three months of his confinement at the Hotel Phoenix in Somerset he managed to keep up his spirits in spite of the suffering and loneliness, and to break the tedium of the dull days he commenced the study of French without the aid of either grammar or dictionary. At last, in January, 1840, he thought himself strong enough to proceed to New York; but it was in the midst of winter and he had to be driven in a sleigh over the Alleghany Mountains. This occasioned considerable delay, and when he at length arrived at his destination he found that his ship had already sailed. He then made his way to his home in Virignia to recuperate his health and strength under the apprehension that his injury might be so serious as to incapacitate him for further active service in the navy.

During the long weeks in Ohio he had been greatly troubled with these fears and had considered gravely what he might do in the future. He had begun then to think seriously of resorting to the pen, and after his return home this notion "to take to books and be learned" began to take more definite shape in his mind, though he was greatly discouraged at his ignorance and confused by the wilderness of subjects from which to choose. He did not, however, wish to give the impression that he was shirking active service; so he made application on March 14, 1840 to Secretary of the Navy Paulding for any duty which he could perform in his present condition, "service on crutches" as he expressed it. This, of course, was not granted him, and thus relieved temporarily from active service, he began the writing of his "Scraps from the Lucky Bag", a series of magazine articles which were soon to make his name very widely known.

In the summer of 1838, Maury had written five articles for the Richmond *Whig and Public Advertiser* under the *nom de plume* of "Harry Bluff, U.S. Navy". His feelings were at that time raw over the outcome of the Exploring Expedition, and in these fearless, straightforward articles he bitterly criticised the former Secretary of the Navy Dickerson for his inefficiency and called upon his successor, Secretary Paulding, to restore to the navy its former prestige. The appointment of Wilkes to command the expedition was handled without gloves. "There was", wrote Maury, "a cunning little Jacob who had campaigned in Washington a full term of seven years. More prodigal than Laban, you (Secretary of War, Joel R. Poinsett) gave him, for a single term, both the Rachel and the Leah of his heart. A junior lieutenant with scarcely enough service at sea to make him familiar with the common routine of duty on board a man-of-war, and with one or two short interruptions, a

sinecurist on shore for the last fifteen years, he was lifted
over the heads of many laborious and meritorious officers,
and placed by you in the command of the Exploring
Expedition in violation of law".

Maury wrote, in December of the same year, seven
more articles for this newspaper, hiding his identity by
inscribing them "From Will Watch to his old messmate
Harry Bluff".   In these he went further still into details
as to the inefficiency of the administration of the navy,
dealing especially with the waste connected with the
building and repairing of ships, the need for a system of
rules and regulations in the navy, and the advisability of
establishing a naval school.   As to the latter, he wrote,
"There is not, in America, a naval school that deserves
the name, or that pretends to teach more than the mere
rudiments of navigation. . . . Why are not steps
taken to have our officers educated and fitted for this
high responsibility?   The idea of a naval academy has
been ridiculed.   This may be the fault of Congress; I
will not lay the censure at the wrong door—but the Department has been equally inattentive to providing the
young officers with the proper means of learning even
practical seamanship".

These "Harry Bluff" and "Will Watch" articles, together with one other on "Navy Matters" by "Brandywine" which also appeared in the *Whig* at this time and
reveals Maury's authorship through its style, contained
the germs of the ideas which he more fully developed in his
"Scraps from the Lucky Bag".   This series of articles
on the need of reform in the conduct of naval affairs
appeared in the *Southern Literary Messenger* during the
years 1840 and 1841, under Maury's former pseudonym
of "Harry Bluff".   The navy was then in a condition of

dry rot, and the time was ripe for some courageous person
to awaken the country to a realization of the true state of
affairs and to point out the reforms that were needed.
Maury's former experience in the naval service and his
present enforced leisure led him to take up the task,
which he performed with a brilliancy and a degree of
success that was far beyond even his own expectation
and gave him a national reputation.

His choice of the *Messenger* as the medium for conveying to the public his ideas on maritime subjects had been
made the previous year when there was published in it
an unsigned article, entitled "A Scheme for Rebuilding
Southern Commerce: Direct Trade with the South".
In this he first emphasized the importance of the Great
Circle route for steamers between English and American
ports and pointed out how the *Great Western* on her first
voyage might have saved 260 miles by using such a route
and thus have cut down the time of her passage by about
one whole day. Maury claimed afterwards that after
the appearance of his article a work on navigation was
published in England and that one of its chief recommendations was its chapter on "great circle sailing". Its
author was rewarded with a prize from the Royal Geographical Society, and the work itself was extensively
patronized by the Board of Admiralty, a copy of which
they ordered to be supplied to each of the British men-of-
war in commission.

The significance of the title, "Scraps from the Lucky
Bag", is indicated by the following introductory parody,
which enumerates the contents of a lucky bag on shipboard:

> "Shoe of middy and waister's sock,
> Wing of soldier and idler's frock.

Purser's slops and topman's hat,
Boatswain's call and colt and cat,
Belt that on the berth-deck lay,
In the Lucky Bag find their way;
Gaiter, stock, and red pompoon,
Sailor's pan, his pot and spoon,
Shirt of cook and trowser's duck,
Kid and can and 'doctor's truck',
And all that's lost and found on board
In the Lucky Bag's always stored."

It was a well-chosen and apt title, which enabled
Maury to treat in the same article of various matters
more or less unrelated. Among the various topics that
he touched upon was, first, the desirability of having
grades in the navy higher than those of captain, to
correspond with those in foreign navies. He also declared that there should be a larger force on the coast of
Africa to put down the traffic in slaves, and more warships in the Pacific to support American commerce with
China and to protect American fishermen on the whaling
grounds. Thus prophetically did he portray the future
of American trade on that ocean: "If you have a map of
the world at hand, turn to it and, placing your finger at
the mouth of the Columbia River, consider its geographical position and the commercial advantages which, at
some day not far distant, that point will possess. To the
south, in one unbroken line, lie several thousand miles of
coast indented with rich markets of Spanish America—
to the west, Asiatic Russia and China are close at hand—
between the south and west are New Holland and
Polynesia; and within good marketable distance are all
the groups and clusters of islands that stud the ocean,
from Cape Horn to the Cape of Good Hope, from Asia
to America. Picture to yourself civilization striding the
Rocky Mountains, and smiling down upon the vast and

fruitful regions beyond, and calculate, if you can, the important and future greatness of that point to a commercial and enterprising people. Yet the first line in the hydrography of such a point remains to be run. It has been more than twenty years since an American man-of-war so much as looked into the mouth of the Columbia River. Upon what more important service could a small force be dispatched than to survey and bring home correct charts of that river and its vicinity?"

He then pointed out the unpreparedness of the country for war, and dwelt upon how the United States was forced weakly to acquiesce in the blockading of Mexico and the La Plata by France, and make no protest at the strengthening of her forts on the Great Lakes by England who was thus violating her treaty with this government. The navy should, he declared, experiment with steam vessels of war, and Pensacola and some point on the coast of Georgia or the eastern coast of Florida should be fortified. Turning then to personnel, he continued: "It takes something more than spars and guns, and walls of wood to constitute a navy. These are only the body—the arms and legs without the thews and sinews. It requires the muscle of the brawny seaman, and the spirit of the well-trained officer to impart life and motion to such a body, to give vigor and energy to the whole system".

A real system of education for the navy should be devised. The army, he said, had a Military Academy at West Point, "affording the most useful and practical education to be obtained in the country"; while the navy was forced to make out with inefficient schoolmasters on board ship, and the midshipmen secured only a practical knowledge of seamanship, the manipulation of the sextant, a few rules by rote from Bowditch's "Epitome of

Navigation", and a knowledge of right-angled plane trigonometry. Maury claimed that a broader training was needed, and suggested the following subjects as requisite for study: drawing and naval architecture, gunnery and pyrotechny, chemistry and natural history, astronomy, mathematics, natural philosophy, navigation, tactics and discipline, gymnastics, international and maritime law, and languages (one of French, Spanish, or German and "that most difficult, arbitrary, and careful of all languages, the English"). These subjects were to be covered in a four years' course, with a two months' cruise each year, sometimes to foreign waters; while two years at sea after graduation and an examination at the end of that period of service were to be required before a commission in the navy was to be awarded.

At first, Maury proposed merely a school-ship; but a little later after his articles had been received with such favor by the public he declared that his advocacy of a school-ship had been made solely on the grounds of expediency and that he would hail with delight the establishment of a school for the navy anywhere, even on the top of the Rocky Mountains. He thereupon suggested Memphis, Tennessee as a suitable place for the school, on the grounds that the East had the Military Academy and the West should have the naval school, and besides that this would be a favorable place for experimenting on steam vessels on the Mississippi River. Though Maury was by no means the first to suggest the need for such an institution, yet no other person contributed so much as he did towards the education of public opinion and the preparation for the eventual establishment of the Naval Academy. It is with justice, therefore, that he has often been referred to as the father of this famous institution.

Continuing his discussion of the needs of the navy as to personnel, Maury recommended a reorganization and standardization of the number of officers in the various grades and a system of promotion that would keep alive the spirit and ambition of the officers. Surplus officers, he thought, might go into the merchant marine and constitute a naval reserve; while the revenue service should be taken over by the regular navy.

Maury then turned to the question of material and devoted a great deal of attention to the graft and inefficiency connected with the building and repairing of ships. "Honorable legislators", he wrote, "are warned that the evils are deeply seated in the system itself, and are not to be removed by merely the plucking of a leaf, or the lopping off of a limb: the axe must be laid at the root—for nothing short of thorough and complete reorganization will do". His attack was directed particularly against the Board of Navy Commissioners; and when this board attempted a reply, he answered with the most devastating article of the whole series, in which he piled up figures, and multiplied instances of graft and ruinous waste. As a summary, he wrote, "Vessels are built at twice the sum they ought to cost—they are repaired at twice as much as it takes to build—the labor to repair costs three times as much as the labor to construct—the same articles for one ship cost four or five times as much as their duplicates for another—it costs twice as much to *repair* ordnance and stores for a ship as it takes to buy them". Maury advocated in place of this board a bureau system with divided responsibility. The Secretary of the Navy, he thought, should have an assistant under-secretary, who should be a post captain in the navy and have general oversight over the various bureaus. Then promotions would be taken out of politics, and the old saying that "a cruise of a few months in Washington tells more than a three years' cruise at sea in an officer's favor" would lose its significance.

In his attempt to improve conditions in the naval service, Maury had the sympathy of a large number of his brother officers, some of whom gave practical expression to their feeling by clubbing together and having large editions of the "Scraps from the Lucky Bag" printed for free distribution. In the month of July, 1841 there appeared a sketch of Maury in the *Southern Literary Messenger*, in which his name was for the first time connected with the authorship of the articles. It was written by a "Brother Officer", who said that the "Scraps from the Lucky Bag" had produced "an enthusiasm which has not subsided and will not subside until the whole navy is reorganized". Such indeed was the outcome. Congress took up the matter, and many of Maury's suggested reforms were at once instituted, while practically everything that he contended for was eventually adopted for the naval service. So famous did Maury become through the publication of these articles that the President was urged to place him at the head of the Navy Department; and at one time President Tyler had actually made up his mind to make him his Secretary of the Navy in spite of the fact that he was then but a lieutenant.

In November, 1841, Maury made another request for active service. In order that his family and friends might not defeat his purpose, he went to Richmond and from there wrote to Secretary of the Navy George E.

Badger, suggesting that he was able to perform any of the lighter duties at sea which did not call for. much bodily exercise, and requesting that he be appointed flag-lieutenant in the Pacific Squadron under Commofore Jones, who had signified a desire to have him in this post. His purpose, however, was thwarted by Judge John T. Lomax, a warm personal friend, who wrote to the Secretary and enclosed a certificate from three of the best physicians of Fredericksburg to the effect that Maury was in no condition for life on board ship; and as a consequence he was retained on the list of those "waiting orders".

After the completion of his "Scraps from the Lucky Bag", Maury continued to write for the *Southern Literary Messenger*; he rendered editorial service to Mr. White, the owner of the magazine, during the year 1842, and was virtually the editor during the first eight months of 1843 after White's death. He contributed also to the *Army and Navy Chronicle* and the *Southern Quarterly Review* of Charleston.

His "Letters to Clay" in the *Messenger* under the pseudonym of "Union Jack" strongly advocated the establishment of a national dockyard at Memphis, government subsidies for the building of steam packets as England and France were doing, a national steamboat canal from the upper Mississippi River to the Lakes for defense against Canada in case of war with Great Britain, a strong naval establishment at some place on the Atlantic seaboard south of Norfolk, and the making of Pensacola a veritable "Toulon on the Mediterranean". The following year, 1842, he took up in the same journal the question of the right of Great Britain to visit and search American ships in the "suspicious" latitudes off

Africa in the endeavor to suppress the slave trade. He was against according this right to England because of the temptation to use the power involved in an arbitrary manner greatly to the injury of American commerce, and he was of the opinion that it was merely an attempt, under the pretext of supporting the "Christian League" or Quintuple Alliance, to revive the old claim of England's right to violate sailors' rights and the freedom of the seas, principles fought for in the War of 1812. He referred, in passing, to the tense feeling against Great Britain on account of the Maine Boundary dispute, and the desire, on the part of many, even for war. "On the contrary", he wrote, "I should view a war between the United States and Great Britain as one of the greatest calamities, except a scourge direct from the hand of God, that could befall my country". But he added, "In the navy, there is but one sentiment and one feeling on this subject; it is, avert war, honorably if you can; if not, let it come: right or wrong, the stars and stripes shall not be disgraced on the ocean".

He too was opposed to the slave trade, and thought that the United States would be glad to coöperate with Great Britain and furnish warships for the purpose; but he doubted the sincerity of England, and referred pointedly to the "hosts of murdered Chinese who prefer instant death at the mouth of British cannon to the slow poison of a British drug",—the opium that was at that time being forced upon them by the British government. His conclusion was this: "When the British government shall cease to sell its captured slaves—when it shall abandon its intrigues for the right of search which has done the Africans so much more harm than good—and shall advocate some such practical plan as this (coöperation) for the suppression of the slave trade, then and not till then will we give the 'old country' credit for motives of humanity and a sincere desire to succor the slave".

These were the last articles that Maury wrote before he was appointed to an office of great potential importance, which was to afford the appropriate place for the complete flowering of his peculiar genius. This appointment was given to him largely because of his writings; namely, his "New Theoretical and Practical Treatise on Navigation", "Scraps from the Lucky Bag", and other magazine articles. It might be said, therefore, that though he had been faithful in the performance of all the duties of his profession and, courageous as he was, would almost certainly have distinguished himself in warfare, yet up to this point in his career the pen, as an instrument for acquiring fame, had indeed been mightier than the sword.

CHAPTER IV

His Astronomical Work

Maury took charge, on July 1, 1842, of the Depot of Charts and Instruments, of which he had just been made the superintendent by Secretary of the Navy Upshur. This depot had been established by the Navy Department in 1830, and Lieutenants Goldsborough, Wilkes, and Gilliss in succession had been its former superintendents. Wilkes had moved it from the western part of the city to Capitol Hill probably, as has been suggested, that its virtues and its needs might the more readily be noticed by Congress. Be that as it may, Congress passed an act on August 31, 1842, appropriating the sum of $35,000 for supplying adequate buildings and equipment for the depot. On the same day was passed another act, which dissolved the Board of Navy Commissioners that had ruled the navy for twenty-seven years and had recently been attacked so forcefully by Maury, and established the Bureau System in its place. The Depot of Charts and Instruments, accordingly, was placed under the Bureau of Ordnance and Hydrography.

Immediately after becoming superintendent, Maury moved the depot to a building between 24th and 25th Streets, N. W., known formerly as 2222–24 Pennsylvania Avenue, and to the rather limited accommodations here he brought his family. Meanwhile a new building was being constructed on a reservation at 23d and E Streets, N. W., where the Naval Medical School is now located,— a site covering about seventeen acres which had been reserved by General Washington for a great university.

An Engraving of the United States Naval Observatory Buildings as They Appeared When Maury Was Superintendent about 1845

From an engraving in the title page of "Astronomical and Meteorological Observations Made during the Year 1875, at the
U. S. Naval Observatory," 1878.

This new building was to be of brick, in the form of a square about 50 feet by 50, surmounted by a dome 23 feet in diameter, with wings to the south, east, and west. Later, in 1847, the superintendent's residence was constructed and connected with the main building by an extension of the east wing.

The name of the institution varied. As the Depot of Charts and Instruments it was officially known from 1830 to 1844; but for the next ten years the names Naval Observatory and National Observatory were used indiscriminately, sometimes even in the same publication. In December, 1854, the Secretary of the Navy instructed that it should henceforth be called the United States Naval Observatory and Hydrographical Office, and as such it was known until the establishment of the Hydrographic Office as a separate division in 1866. Since that date the official name of the institution has been the United States Naval Observatory.

Near the close of September, 1844, the Observatory was reported to be completed, and on October 1 Maury was ordered to take charge with a staff of line officers and professors of mathematics of the navy, and civilian professors. Lieutenant James M. Gilliss, Maury's predecessor, had been greatly interested in astronomy, especially that field of the science having to do with navigation, and it was largely through his exertions that the necessary legislation had been passed making possible a building, adapted not merely to the housing of charts and instruments but suitable as well for astronomical observations. He had been sent to Europe to consult about the purchasing of instruments for the new Observatory, and there were those who thought that he should have been made its first superintendent.

However scantily informed Maury may have been in the beginning as to the great advance in astronomical science recently made in Europe, his great energy and native ability soon enabled him to overcome any such handicaps. He assisted with his own hands in the installation of the instruments, in which he took great delight, writing that the Great Refraction Circle was such an exquisite piece of machinery and so beautiful that he would like to wear it round his neck as an ornament. He was constantly endeavoring to secure better and larger instruments, and wrote with pride when the Observatory, as far as equipment was concerned, became the second most important in the world and needed only a larger telescope to make it the very first of all. Maury quickly saw the value of the Electro-Chronograph, invented by John Locke of Cincinnati, in determining longitude with the aid of the magnetic telegraph, seeing that it would practically double the number of observations that one observer could make; and it was largely through him that Congress was persuaded to appropriate the $10,000 necessary for installing the instrument at the Observatory.

Maury was, moreover, by no means a mere figurehead in the making of astronomical observations, but soon mastered the details of this work which might have been left wholly to his subordinates. During the first two years he was the principal observer with the equatorial, and it is interesting to note how often his name appears as the observer in the published extracts from the notebooks of the Observatory. That he had much more than a mere passing interest in astronomy is evident from the following account of his emotions during an astronomical observation: "To me the simple passage through the transit instrument of a star across the meridian is the height of astronomical sublimity. At the dead hour of the night, when the world is hushed in sleep and all is still; when there is not a sound to be heard save the dead beat escapement of the clock, counting with hollow voice the footsteps of time in his ceaseless round, I turn to the Ephemeris and find there, by calculation made years ago, that when that clock tells a certain hour, a star which I never saw will be in the field of the telescope for a moment, flit through, and then disappear. The instrument is set;—I look; the star, mute with eloquence that gathers sublimity from the silence of the night, comes smiling and dancing into the field, and at the instant predicted even to the fraction of a second it makes its transit and is gone! With emotions too deep for the organs of speech, the heart swells out with unutterable anthems; we then see that there is harmony in the heavens above; and though we cannot hear, we feel the 'music of the spheres'".[1]

Maury's first volume of astronomical observations, the first indeed to be issued from an American observatory, appeared in 1846. Though this was pioneer work, it was important enough to cause one of the most distinguished astronomers of Europe to conclude that it had placed the American observatory in the front rank with the oldest and best institutions of the kind in Europe. In the appendix to this volume, Maury gives very generous credit and praise to his helpers, among whom were at this time the distinguished mathematicians Hubbard, Keith, and Coffin; but he adds that he considers himself

---

[1] From "The National Observatory" read by Maury before the Virginia Historical Society. It was copied from *The Historical Register* in the *Southern Literary Messenger* of May, 1849.

alone responsible for the accuracy of the work as nothing had been published until it had passed his supervision and approval.

A very ambitious work which Maury began during the year 1845 was a catalogue of the stars. The aim was to cover every point of space in the visible heavens with telescopes, get the position of every star, cluster, and nebula, and record both magnitude and color, with the angle of position and the distance of binary stars together with descriptions and drawings of all clusters and nebulæ. No astronomical work on such an extensive scale had ever before been executed or even attempted, though the value and importance of it were manifold and difficult of full estimation. Maury wrote that it was his intention to make a contribution to astronomy that would be worthy of the nation and the age, and to so execute the undertaking that future astronomers would value it so highly as to say that such a star was not visible in the heavens at the date of the Washington Catalogue because it is not recorded therein.

An interesting example of the extremely practical value of such a catalogue came up in connection with Leverrier's discovery of the planet Neptune. In the autumn of 1846, after the discovery of this planet, Maury ordered one of his observers to trace its path backwards to see if some astronomer had observed it and entered it as a fixed star. On February 1, 1847, the observer, Sears Cook Walker, gave a list of fourteen stars from Lalande's catalogue in his "Histoire Celeste", where Neptune should have been approximately in May, 1795. Professor Hubbard was then directed by Maury to examine with the equatorial, and he found on the night of February 4 that the suspected star was missing.

It was concluded, therefore, that Lalande had observed and recorded Neptune as a fixed star on the nights of May 8 and 10, 1795. This discovery enabled astronomers to compute the new planet's orbit from observations extending over a period of fifty years.

The work on this catalogue was carried forward industriously for several years, but the results were not ready to be published in the volume of observations for the year 1846 because of the continual drafts on the personnel of the Observatory for sea duty, which made it impossible for the computers to keep pace with the observers. Eventually, Maury was compelled to abandon the hope of ever finishing a complete catalogue of the stars, as at first planned. The observations continued to be made, however, and by January of 1855 the number of stars which had been so observed reached the grand total of 100,000; but these results were not published until 1873, long after Maury's superintendency had come to a close. Maury would never have undertaken such an ambitious work, if he had realized the Herculean labor involved in the cataloguing of all the stars down to the 10th magnitude in all the heavens from 45° south to the North Pole, a colossal undertaking that was entirely beyond the capacity of any one observatory to accomplish in a generation.

The appearance of the second volume of astronomical observations was delayed because of the inroads made on Maury's staff by the demands of the Mexican War. Then when the work was on the point of being published it was destroyed by a fire which burned the printing office. So the volume did not appear until the year 1851; and as the years went by publications fell further and further behind the observations. There is no doubt but that Maury was greatly handicapped by the assignment of officers to the Observatory for irregular periods, and by the reduction of the number of his mathematicians as time went by. There was, besides, the hydrographical work of his office which made constantly increasing demands on him and his staff. When he was forced by this lack in personnel to make a choice between the more complete development of astronomical observations on the one hand, and hydrographical and meteorological research on the other, he wisely chose the latter as of more immediate and practical value to the United States, and indeed to the entire world.

Courtesy of "The Journal of American History," Vol. IV, Number 3 (1910).

DECORATIONS CONFERRED UPON MAURY

(From reader's left to right) First and fourth are the obverse and reverse of the decoration of the Tower and Sword conferred by the King of Portugal. Second is the diamond pin presented by Maximilian of Austria. Third and sixth are the obverse and reverse of the decoration, Cross of the Order of Dannebrog, given by the King of Denmark. Fifth is the pearl and diamond brooch presented to Mrs. Maury by the Czar of Russia, see page 65. (Maury was also made a commander of the Legion of Honor, and a knight of the Order of St. Anne by the Czar of Russia.)

CHAPTER V

HIS WIND AND CURRENT CHARTS

At the top of all the pilot charts issued by the Hydrographic Office of the Navy Department are written these words: "Founded upon the researches made and the data collected by Lieutenant M. F. Maury, U. S. Navy". This is an appropriate memorial to Maury's most practical contribution to science,—that which has given him the name "Pathfinder of the Seas".

For a long time he had recognized the need for charts showing the winds and currents of the sea at different seasons; and it will be remembered that, when he was sailing master of the *Falmouth*, 1831–1833, he was first made to realize how little of the nautical experience of other sailors could be taken advantage of by one about to set out on a long voyage. On the way down to Rio in this ship he first conceived the idea of a wind and current chart; but he had no opportunity to make practical investigations into the meteorology of the sea until the year 1842, when he was placed in charge of the Depot of Charts and Instruments.

He had been in this office but a short time when he set about examining the old log books which had been stored away as so much rubbish by the Navy Department. By the middle of the year 1843, these investigations had proved so illuminating that he was able to write a paper, which was read before the National Institute, on "Blank Charts on Board Public Cruisers". According to his plan, these charts were to have parallels and meridians showing the latitude and longitude laid down upon them, and the commanders of ships were to be requested to lay off on them the tracks of their vessels every day, and indicate as well the time of the year, the direction of the winds, the force and set of the currents, and all other phenomena having a bearing on the navigation of the seas on which they sailed. Sailing directions, Maury declared in this address, are now not a written branch of navigation but merely a matter of tradition among seamen. As to his contemplated chart, he boldly asserted that short passages are not due to luck and that "this chart proposes nothing less than to *blaze a way* through the winds of the sea by which the navigator may find the best paths at all seasons".

Not having at that time made a name for himself as a scientist, Maury thought it wise to seek the support of the National Institute, and asked that a committee be appointed from its members to wait upon Secretary of the Navy Upshur and invite his coöperation in authorizing that these charts be kept on all public cruisers. Such coöperation was, after a fashion, granted, and Maury drew up a letter of instructions at the request of the Secretary. But as not much political capital was to be made of it, the matter ended with the issuing of a set of instructions to Commodore Biddle who was on the point of sailing for China in the *Columbus*. Maury then asked permission of the Bureau of Ordnance and Hydrography to make a chart of the Atlantic American seaboard. He was ashamed, he wrote, of the meagerness of the contributions of the United States to the general fund of nautical science, and called attention to the fact that even the charts used by an American man-of-war in making her way up the Chesapeake Bay toward Washington had to be secured from the English Admiralty, and that, if it were not for the Nautical Almanac of England or some other nation, absent American ships could not find their way home and those in port could not lift their anchors and grope to sea with any certainty of finding their way back again.

At about the same time Maury began the compilation of a chart of the North Atlantic for the purpose of laying down upon it the tracks of vessels in all seasons of the year, with the currents, prevailing winds, temperature of the water, etc. At first, he had the intention of delineating the track of each vessel on the chart but he soon saw that it would be impossible to do so on the scale adopted (one inch to the degree), and he then resorted to the plan of tabulating the results only instead of marking the track. It was not until the autumn of 1847 that his researches, which had then extended over nearly five years, had reached the point where he could publish his first "Wind and Current Chart of the North Atlantic". This chart was founded entirely upon information derived from the old discarded log books of the Navy Department, for he had not then secured much coöperation in the acquiring of new data. Maury compared his work in the "quarry of log books" to that of a sculptor, the single touch of whose chisel does but little; but finally like the completed piece of statuary the charts speak for themselves and stand out before the compiler "eloquent with facts which the philosopher had never dreamed were lurking near".

Early in the year 1848 Maury issued what he called an "Abstract Log for the Use of American Navigators". This was devised to secure the coöperation of navigators in gathering information for perfecting his charts. It contained but ten pages together with some blank forms, and was the very modest beginning of what he afterwards issued as "Sailing Directions", which eventually grew to the enormous size of 1257 pages in two volumes in quarto. The purpose of the little pamphlet was to interpret the meaning and the significance of the wind and current chart which had recently been issued, and to furnish instructions to navigators for the proper keeping of the abstract log on their voyages. They were to enter in this log the latitude and longitude every day at noon; the hourly rate of the currents expressed in knots; the variation of the compass; the reading of the thermometer, in both air and water, at nine o'clock each morning; the state of the barometer just before, during, and just after a gale of wind with the changes and time of changes in the direction of the wind during the gale; careful entries as to the direction and force of the winds every eight hours; and other marine phenomena such as whales, flocks of birds, rains and fogs, etc., etc. When properly filled out, these logs were to be sent to Maury at the Observatory where the information would be tabulated. It was also suggested that tightly corked bottles containing the latitude and longitude, and the date be thrown overboard at stated times, and that such floating bottles be picked up when seen, and the .place and time be carefully noted in the abstract log. Those who agreed to coöperate in these various ways were to receive free of cost a copy of the "Wind and Current Chart of the North Atlantic".

Maury predicted confidently that, by following his directions, the average 55 days' voyage from New York to Rio by the old route might be shortened by from 10 to 15 days. This prediction was fulfilled by the barque *W. H. D. C. Wright* of Baltimore, which early in 1848 went from the Capes of Virginia to Rio in 35 days and returned in 40 days, by following Maury's directions. This created considerable interest in the new charts, and the number of those willing to coöperate in the new research on the sea constantly increased from year to year. Maury had long looked forward to the prospect of no longer being compelled to search through cartloads of manuscripts and dusty log books, kept in years gone by without system and with little or no regard to the facts which he wished to obtain from them, but of having as co-laborers a thousand or more vessels every year engaged in collecting exactly the information required so that it would come to his hands precisely in the form in which it was desired. In this he was not to be disappointed for by the close of the year 1848 he was able to write that his charts were eagerly sought by navigators and that some five or six thousand of them had been distributed during the year to American shipmasters. By no means all of these navigators kept their part of the agreement and sent in to Maury their abstract logs properly filled out; but enough data kept coming in to keep his staff of helpers constantly at work turning out his various charts. By 1851, he could write that more than one thousand ships in all the oceans were observing for him, and that enough material had been collected from abstract logs to make two hundred large manuscript volumes each averaging from two thousand to three thousand days' observations.

These "Wind and Current Charts" included Track Charts, Trade Wind Charts, Pilot Charts, Thermal Charts, Storm and Rain Charts, and Whale Charts. The Track Charts showed the frequented parts of the ocean, the general character of the weather and wind, and the force and direction of the latter at different seasons of the year. The Trade Wind Charts gave the limits, extent, and general characteristics of the trade wind regions, together with their neighboring zones of calms. The Pilot Charts showed in every square of fifteen degrees the direction of the wind for sixteen points of the compass that would probably be found in that square during each month of the year, the results being based upon the number of times the wind was reported to have been from that direction in former years. The Thermal Charts recorded the temperature of the surface of the ocean wherever and whenever it had been observed, the different temperatures being distinguished by colors and symbols in such a manner that mere inspection of the chart showed the temperature for any month. The Storm and Rain Charts demonstrated in every square of five degrees the number of observations that had been made for each month, the number of days in which there had been rain, a calm, fog, lightning and thunder, or a storm and the quarter from which it had blown. The Whale Charts, finally, showed where whales were most hunted, in what years and months they had been most frequently found, whether in shoals or as stragglers, and whether sperm or right whales.

Though the coöperation which Maury enjoyed was an extensive one, he was still not satisfied, and as early as 1851 he conceived the idea of a universal system of meteorological observations on both land and sea. Through the advice of British scientists, he decided to confine his system, for the time being, only to the sea, though he was afterwards to regret such a curtailment of his original scheme. With the authority of Secretary of the Navy William A. Graham, to whom Maury was greatly indebted for very generous support in furthering his ambitious project, he set to work through diplomatic representatives of foreign countries at Washington to interest as many meteorologists as possible in the convening of an international meteorological conference. The United States also was asked to coöperate, through letters which Maury sent to the various Cabinet Members, heads of the Coast Survey, the Bureau of Engineers, and the Smithsonian Institute, and other scientists. Paris was at first considered to be a suitable place for the meeting; but eventually Brussels was chosen, and the following nations accepted the invitation to send representatives: Belgium, Denmark, France, Great Britain, Netherlands, Norway, Portugal, Russia, Sweden, and the United States.

Maury, as the representative of the United States, sailed from New York on July 23, 1853, by way of England. Upon landing at Liverpool, he was invited to address the merchants in the City Hall on the subject of the uniform plan of observation at sea, and the following month he spoke to the underwriters and ship-owners of London at Lloyd's on the same subject. These speeches produced a more cordial coöperation on the part of the British government which had previously been rather lukewarm in its attitude toward the undertaking.

The conference was convened at the residence of the Minister of the Interior in Brussels on August 23, 1853, and Jacques Adolphe Lambert Quetelet, Director of the Royal Observatory of Belgium, was made its president. Maury was requested to direct the proceedings of the conference, but he declined the honor. He was then asked by the president to state the purposes of the meeting.

and after his short introductory address President Quetelet proposed that the conference pass a vote of thanks to Maury and record their gratitude for the "enlightened zeal and earnestness" he had displayed in the important and useful work which formed the subject of their deliberations. This, of course, was unanimously passed. The discussions went on daily with the greatest harmony, until the close of the conference on September 8. The results were the adoption of an abstract log for the use of the men-of-war of all nations and also one for all merchantmen to use in the system of coöperative observations. Full explanatory notes for the keeping of these logs in such a way as to cover all the phenomena of the ocean were agreed upon, and the hope was expressed that these abstract logs might enjoy in time of war the same immunity that was accorded to vessels engaged in discovery or other scientific research.

The Brussels Conference was an unqualified success, and Maury was very enthusiastic over the new chapter of Marine Meteorology which was about to be opened in the volume of Nature. "Rarely before", he wrote somewhat later, "has there been such a sublime spectacle presented to the scientific world: all nations agreeing to unite and coöperate in carrying out one system of philosophical research with regard to the sea. Though they may be enemies in all else, here they are to be friends. Every ship that navigates the high seas, with these charts and blank abstract logs on board, may henceforth be regarded as a floating observatory, a temple of science".[1]

Soon after the conference, Prussia, Spain, Sardinia,

[1] From "Introduction", p. xiii, to Maury's *Physical Geography of the Sea*, 1855.

the free city of Hamburg, the republic of Bremen, Chile, Austria, and Brazil, all joined the enterprise; and the Pope established honorary flags of distinction for the ships of the papal states, which could be awarded only to those vessels which kept the abstract logs of the Brussels Conference.

Maury took with him on this mission to Europe his two eldest daughters and their cousins Ellen Herndon and Ellen Maury, who were dubbed by acclamation on the steamer the "Magpie Club". In England the party was invited to Wrottesley Hall near Wolverhampton, by Lord Wrottesley, then President of the Royal and Astronomical Societies, with whom Maury had corresponded for several years. Before returning to America, he and his "Magpie Club" traveled in France, Holland, and Germany, and visited the great scientist Humboldt, whose "Cosmos" had greatly influenced Maury's scientific ideas.

Back at home again, Maury took up his work with renewed energy, and with the data which came in, through the greatly increased coöperation, from all quarters and in many different languages, he revised his charts of the North and South Atlantic, and of the North and South Pacific, and then charted the Indian Ocean as well. Not only was the route to Rio definitely decreased by one fourth, but also other passages began to be shortened with the accompanying saving for all the men and commerce that used Maury's suggested routes. The gold rush to California, which began in 1849, vastly increased the shipping from the Atlantic ports of the United States to San Francisco. Time then became a more important element in that passage than ever before, and in 1850 clipper ships were launched for this particular trade, with the object of making the voyage as short as possible. It was, therefore, a splendid opportunity for putting Maury's charts to the test, and the practical results of his new sailing directions soon displayed themselves.

Before his charts came to be used, the average passage from New York to San Francisco was about 180 days, but by the year 1855 the average passage between those ports for the year round had been reduced to 133 days. Moreover, there were dozens of clipper ships which, under Maury's directions, made the voyage in 110 days or even less. The record was made in 1851 by the *Flying Cloud*, which fairly flew over the passage in 89 days and 21 hours, during one day making the extraordinary distance of $433\frac{1}{2}$ statute miles or sailing at the rate of 18 statute miles per hour. This exploit was celebrated with great rejoicing in San Francisco, because the inhabitants felt that they had been brought so much nearer to their old homes in the East.

Under the circumstances it was but natural that there should be races among the clipper ships. The route from New York to San Francisco became the great race-course of the ocean, fifteen thousand miles in length. As Maury wrote, "Some of the most glorious trials of speed and prowess that the world ever witnessed; among ships that 'walk the waters', have taken place over it. Here the modern clipper ship—the noblest work that has ever come from the hands of man—has been sent, guided by the lights of science, to contend with the elements, to outstrip steam, and astonish the world".[2] There was the great race in 1851 of the *Raven*, the *Typhoon*, and the *Sea Witch*, which was won by the first-

[2] "Physical Geography of the Sea", 1855, p. 263.

mentioned in 105 days, though the year before this same ship had made the run in 97 days.

Another famous race was run during the winter of 1852–1853, and the ships which engaged in it were the *Wild Pigeon, John Gilpin, Flying Fish*, and *Trade Wind*. These ships, as were those in the former race, were all furnished with Maury's charts.   After a most interesting and exciting race, the *Flying Fish* won in just 92 days and 4 hours, though the *John Gilpin* was a close second, making the passage in 93 days and 20 hours.   In commenting on these results, Maury wrote, "Here are ships sailing on different days, bound over a trackless waste of ocean for some fifteen thousand miles or more, and depending alone on the fickle winds of heaven, as they are called, to waft them along; yet, like travelers on the land bound upon the same journey, they pass and repass, fall in with and recognize each other by the way; and what, perhaps, is still more remarkable is the fact that these ships should each, throughout that great distance and under the wonderful vicissitudes of climates, winds, and currents, which they encountered, have been so skillfully navigated that, in looking back at their management, now that what is past is before me, I do not find a single occasion, except the one already mentioned, on which they could have been better handled. . . . . Am I far wrong, therefore, when I say that the present state of our knowledge, with regard to the physical geography of the sea, has enabled the navigator to blaze his way among the winds and currents of the sea, and so mark his path that others, using his signs as fingerboards, may follow in the same track?"[3]

The degree of exactness which Maury's knowledge of

[3] "Sailing Directions", sixth edition (1854), pp. 725–730.

the sea had reached is best illustrated by the incident of the *San Francisco*. This ship, bound from New York to San Francisco with a regiment of soldiers on board, was disabled in a hurricane on the day before Christmas, 1853 while crossing the Gulf Stream about 300 miles from Sandy Hook. Her position on the following day, and the next day after that, was reported by passing vessels which were, however, unable to render her assistance. Maury was then asked by the Secretary of the Navy to calculate her position for the assistance of the two relief ships which were to be dispatched in search of the unfortunate vessel. Although three other ships, the *Kilby*, the *Three Bells*, and the *Antarctic*, fell in with the wreck and rescued the remainder of her passengers, after 179 men had been washed overboard, yet it is an astonishing fact that Maury had so accurately guided the two searching revenue cutters that one of them went within sight of the spot where the drifting vessel had shortly before been found.

There was still another important passage that Maury aided materially in shortening. This was the voyage from England to Australia and New Zealand. He opposed the British Admiralty route which passed near the Cape of Good Hope, and advised ships to sail 600 to 800 miles further westward and then to continue southward until they reached the prevailing strong westerly winds which drove the clippers onward at a tremendous rate. He advised them, when homeward bound, to continue in those "brave west winds" and return by way of Cape Horn. A voyage out to Australia and home again, accordingly, encircled the globe. Whereas by the old route it had taken about 120 days each way on the average, by Maury's new route the passage for American sailings was decreased by one third and that for the British by about one fifth.

This shortening of ships' passages amounted to a vast saving to the commerce of the world. It was estimated that the annual saving to British commerce in the Indian Ocean alone, from Maury's charts and sailing directions, amounted to $1,000,000 at least, and the amount saved to British commerce in all seas reached the stupendous sum of $10,000,000 annually. As to the United States, it has been conservatively estimated that the saving for the outward voyage alone from her Atlantic and California ports to those of South America, Australia, China, and the East Indies amounted to $2,250,000 per annum.

For many years the scientific world rang with Maury's praise, though there were, of course, some detractors. In referring to these "closet men of science" who claimed that he pushed his speculations oftentimes beyond the limits which the facts before him would authorize a prudent and cautious investigator to go, he wrote that the true problem with which he had to deal was to use his opportunities so as to produce the greatest good to the greatest numbers, and that he was willing to be judged by the fruits of his labor. Furthermore, he announced again and again in his "Sailing Directions" the following rule by which his investigations had always been guided: "To keep the mind unbiassed by theories and speculations; never to have any wish that an investigation would result in favor of this view in preference to that, and never to attempt by premature speculation to anticipate the results of investigation, but always to trust to the observations".

In spite of his great achievements, Maury's own countrymen were rather backward about rewarding him.

The University of North Carolina conferred upon him an A.M. degree in 1847 and a LL.D. in 1852, and Columbia University made him a Doctor of Laws in 1854. A. A. Low and Brothers of New York named one of their clipper barques in his honor in 1855. But the most substantial reward bestowed upon him in the United States came in 1853, when the merchants and underwriters of New York presented him a fine silver service and a purse of $5000 in recognition for what he had done for the commerce of that great port. Six years later, a testimonial signed by 363 different American shipowners, masters, and merchants was sent to him as an expression of their "personal regard and esteem".

The reports of the various Secretaries of the Navy from 1850 to 1855 referred in the highest terms of appreciation to the hydrographical work which Maury was doing. Secretary Graham went so far as to write, "Indeed, I doubt whether the triumphs of navigation and the knowledge of the sea, achieved under your superintendence of the Observatory, will not contribute as much to an effective naval service and to the national fame as the brilliant trophies of our arms". Still, notwithstanding this official praise, Maury was kept in the rank of lieutenant, and an attempt made in the Senate in January, 1855 to secure an appropriation of $25,000, as "some substantial evidence of the appreciation of the benefits he has, by his labors, conferred upon his country", came to nought; and a short time thereafter he was treated with the greatest cruelty by the Navy Department which placed him for a time in official disgrace and reduced his pay to $1200 per annum.

Abroad, on the contrary, Maury received almost universal recognition, and the rulers of Europe seemed to vie with each other in conferring medals and decorations upon him. Up to the time of the outbreak of the Civil War, he had been made a member of some 45 learned societies, about 20 of which were in foreign countries. He was made a knight of the Order of Dannebrog by the King of Denmark in 1856, and the following year a knight of the Order of St. Anne by the Czar of Russia and a commander of the Legion of Honor by the Emperor of France; while in 1859 he had conferred upon him the Order of the Tower and Sword by the King of Portugal. Moreover, between the years of 1854 and 1859 gold medals were presented to him by the rulers of Norway and Sweden, Prussia, the republic of Bremen, Holland, Austria, Sardinia, and France; and in addition a medal of honor was awarded him for his charts at the Paris Universal Exhibition of 1855, and only the year before the beginning of the Civil War the Pope sent him a set of thirteen beautiful silver medals. There were two gold medals from Prussia; namely, the medal designed for distinguished works of science and the Cosmos Medal, which had been struck by the King of Prussia to honor Humboldt upon the publication of his "Cosmos" and which was given to Maury because of the warm personal friendship that had long existed between the two great scientists.

Thus was Maury's resourcefulness and perseverance in investigating the winds and currents of the sea and in presenting the results of his research in a practical form for the use of the mariners of the world crowned with success; and whatever the future might hold in store for him, he must have then realized that he had gained for himself an entrance into that small company of the world's most distinguished scientists.

CHAPTER VI

His Physical Geography of the Sea

Maury's investigations of the winds and currents of the sea led him into researches connected with all the phenomena of the ocean, the results of which were so extensive and so valuable as to win for him the right to be called the first great oceanographer of the world.

At the beginning of his work at the Depot of Charts and Instruments, he uncovered in the old log books facts relating to the Gulf Stream, which led him to certain interesting conclusions concerning this great ocean current that had not been previously recognized. In July, 1843 he gave an address before the President, the Corps Diplomatique, and important government officials on "The Gulf Stream and Its Causes", which was reread with certain variations before several different learned societies during the following year. He continued to write such scientific papers on topics bearing on oceanography, while he was engaged in astronomical work and the preparation of his wind and current charts, and these papers, after being delivered before scientific societies, were published by him in the astronomical and meteorological publications of his office. Of particular note were those which appeared in the different editions of his "Sailing Directions" under such titles as "The Influence of the Gulf Stream on the Trade of Charleston", "The Currents of the Sea", "On the Saltness of the Sea", "On the General Circulation of the Atmosphere", "Red Fogs and Sea Dust", "On the Probable Relation between Magnetism and the Circulation of the

COPY OF AN ENGRAVING OF MAURY WHICH HANGS IN THE SUPERINTENDENT'S
OFFICE AT THE UNITED STATES NAVAL OBSERVATORY

Atmosphere", "Of Clouds and Equatorial Cloud Rings", "On the Geological Agency of the Winds", and "Deep Sea Soundings".

The last-mentioned paper was made possible by the coöperation afforded by the government in authorizing in 1849 the Secretary of the Navy to detail three suitable vessels to assist in Maury's wind and current investigations and to order all ships of the navy to coöperate in so far as it was compatible with the public interest.   Maury had long had a desire to explore the bottom of the ocean, and he now saw to it that these ships especially detailed to help him were equipped and thoroughly instructed for making soundings.   The first attempts were made by the schooner *Taney*, under the command of Lieutenant J. C. Walsh, in the autumn of 1849.   But her work was of negligible value, as she succeeded only in losing some 5700 fathoms of line as well as her deep-sea sounding apparatus, and then proved so unseaworthy that she had to be condemned and sent back home under escort.   Later, however, the results secured particularly by Captain Charles T. Platt in the sloop of war *Albany* and by Lieutenants S. P. Lee and O. H. Berryman in the brig *Dolphin* were of great importance.   So extensive was the data regarding soundings at Maury's command by the close of the year 1853 that he was able to publish in the sixth edition of his "Sailing Directions" (1854) ninety pages of matter under the heading of "Physical Geography of the Sea".

This edition of the "Sailing Directions" was brought out by E. C. and J. Biddle of Philadelphia, and when Maury's nephew, Dabney Maury, went to see the publishers about some question connected with its publication, one of the firm called his attention to the fact that Maury's annual report contained materials for a most interesting and valuable book. He warned him that, unless the results of his investigations were thus guarded by a copyright, he would have the chagrin of seeing "some Yankee bookmaker steal his thunder and reap a fortune from it". By the next mail Maury was advised of this. He at once became interested in the undertaking and, with the advice of the Biddles, arrangements were made with Harpers for the publication of such a book. It was begun in the spring of 1854, and finished and ready for the publishers by June 20 of the same year. Maury was of the opinion that it was to be his "*great* work", and time certainly proved that he had not overestimated its importance.

The title of the book was taken from one of the chapter headings in the sixth edition of his "Sailing Directions", and was originally suggested to Maury by Humboldt, who wrote that Maury's investigations had produced an amount of useful information sufficient, in his opinion, to constitute a new department of science which he called the Physical Geography of the Seas. The first edition, published early in the year 1855, contained only 274 pages, and was dedicated "as a token of friendship and a tribute to worth" to George Manning of New York who had been of great assistance to Maury in the distribution of the wind and current charts. In 1861, the eighth and last American edition of 474 pages appeared, and at about the same time an English edition was published by Sampson Low, Son and Company in London. This American edition was dedicated to William C. Hasbrouck of Newburgh, New York "as a token of the friendship and esteem, from boyhood till now, of his former pupil"; while the English edition was inscribed to Lord Wrottesley. The book ran to as many as nineteen editions in England, where it bore the somewhat fuller title of "Physical Geography of the Sea and Its Meteorology". It has been translated into Dutch, German, French, Italian, Spanish, and Norwegian, and has been used as a textbook in several naval schools on the Continent.

As to the contents and general scope of his book, Maury wrote in the introduction, "Under this term will be included a philosophical account of the winds and currents of the sea; of the circulation of the atmosphere and ocean; of the temperature and depth of the sea; of the wonders that are hidden in its depths; and of the phenomena that display themselves at its surface. In short, I shall treat of the economy of the sea and its adaptations—of its salts, its waters, its climates, and its inhabitants, and of whatever there may be of general interest in its commercial uses or industrial pursuits, for all such things pertain to its Physical Geography". It contained also a number of illustrative plates, among which was the first bathymetric map ever made of the North Atlantic Ocean, with contour-lines drawn in at 1000, 2000, 3000, and 4000 fathoms.

Some idea of the nature of the book and of Maury's peculiar style can be best secured by the consideration of some selections taken from it here and there. Those quoted below are, of course, of the nature of "purple patches", for it must not be supposed that there are no dry and uninteresting passages in the book; but they are fairly representative and will probably serve the purpose intended. Maury was the first scientist to make a careful study of the Gulf Stream, and the first chapter of his "Physical Geography of the Sea" is devoted to this mighty ocean current. The reader's interest is gained and his imagination is excited at once by these opening sentences: "There is a river in the ocean. In the severest droughts it never fails, and in the mightiest floods it never overflows. Its banks and its bottom are of cold water, while its current is of warm. The Gulf of Mexico is its fountain, and its mouth is in the Arctic Seas. It is the Gulf Stream. There is in the world no other such majestic flow of waters. Its current is more rapid than the Mississippi or the Amazon, and its volume more than a thousand times greater".

In the chapter on the "Influence of the Gulf Stream upon Climates" is the followng striking passage on whales and other animals of the sea: "Now, the Western Islands is the great place of resort for whales: and at first there is something curious to us in the idea that the Gulf of Mexico is the harvest-field, and the Gulf Stream the gleaner which collects the fruitage planted there, and conveys it thousands of miles off to the hungry whale at sea. But how perfectly in unison is it with the kind and providential care of that great and good Being which feeds the young ravens when they cry, and caters for the sparrow. . . .

"The inhabitants of the ocean are as much the creatures of climate as are those of the dry land; for the same Almighty hand, which decked the lily and cares for the sparrow, fashioned also the pearl and feeds the great whale, and adapted each to the physical conditions by which His providence has surrounded it. Whether of the land or the sea, the inhabitants are all His creatures, subjects of His laws, and agents of His economy. The sea, therefore, we may safely infer, has its offices and duties to perform; so, may we infer, have its currents, and so, too, its inhabitants; consequently, he who undertakes to study its phenomena must cease to regard it as a waste of waters.   He must look upon it as a part of that exquisite machinery by which the harmonies of nature are preserved, and then he will begin to perceive the developments of order and the evidences of design; these make it a most beautiful and interesting subject for contemplation".

This idea of divine order and design occurs again and again in the book like the motive in a piece of music; in fact, Maury, though he did not formally enter the church until late in life, was a very religious man and well read in the Bible, quotations from which appear in his writings by the dozen.   He had very definite ideas about the relation between science and the Bible, and declared that it was his rule never to forget who was the Author of the great volume which Nature spreads out before men, and always to remember that the same Being was the author of the book which revelation holds forth for contemplation.   It was his opinion that, though the works were entirely different, their records were equally true, and that when they bear upon the same point, as they occasionally do, it would be impossible for them to contradict each other.   If the two cannot be reconciled, the fault therefore is in man's weakness and blindness in interpreting them aright.

To return to the "Physical Geography of the Sea", the chapter on the atmosphere contains many noteworthy passages such as the following: ". . . The atmosphere is something more than a shoreless ocean, at the bottom of which he (man) creeps along.   It is an envelope or covering for the dispersion of light and heat over the surface of the earth; it is a sewer into which, with every breath we draw, we cast vast quantities of dead animal matter; it is a laboratory for purification, in which that matter is recompounded, and wrought again into wholesome and healthful shapes; it is a machine for pumping up all the rivers from the sea, and conveying the waters from their fountains on the ocean to their sources in the mountains; it is an inexhaustible magazine, marvellously adapted for many benign and beneficent purposes. . . . To evaporate water enough annually from the ocean to cover the earth, on the average, five feet with rain; to transport it from one zone to another; and to precipitate it in the right places, at suitable times, and in the proportions due, is one of the offices of the grand atmospheric machine. This water is evaporated principally from the torrid zone. Supposing it all to come thence, we shall have, encircling the earth, a belt of ocean three thousand miles in breadth, from which this atmosphere evaporates a layer of water annually sixteen feet in depth. And to hoist up as high as the clouds, and lower again all the water in a lake sixteen feet deep, and three thousand miles broad, and twenty-four thousand long, is the yearly business of this invisible machinery. What a powerful engine is the atmosphere! and how nicely adjusted must be all the cogs, and wheels, and springs, and *compensations* of this exquisite piece of machinery, that it never wears out nor breaks down, nor fails to do its work at the right time, and in the right way".

One other selection, from the chapter on "The Salts of the Sea", will be sufficient as illustrative material. "Take for example", he writes, "the coral islands, reefs, beds, and atolls, with which the Pacific Ocean is studded and garnished. They were built up of materials which a certain kind of insect quarried from the sea water. The currents of the sea ministered to this little insect—they were its *hod carriers*. When fresh supplies of solid matter were wanted for the coral rock upon which the foundations of the Polynesian Islands were laid, those hod carriers brought them in unfailing streams of sea water, loaded with food and building materials for the coralline. The obedient currents thread the widest and deepest seas. They never fail to come at the right time, nor refuse to go; for, unless the currents of the sea were employed to carry off from this insect the waters that have been emptied by it of their lime, and to bring to it others charged with more, it is evident the little creature would have perished for want of food long before its task was half completed. But for currents, it would have been impaled in a nook of the very drop of water in which it was spawned; for it would soon have secreted the lime contained in this drop of water, and then, without the ministering aid of currents to bring it more, it would have perished for the want of food for itself and materials for its edifice; and thus, but for the benign currents which took this exhausted water away, there we perceive this emptied drop would have remained, not only as the grave of the little architect, but as a monument in attestation of the shocking monstrosity that there had been a failure in the sublime system of terrestrial adaptations—that the sea had not been adapted by its Creator to the well-being of all its inhabitants. Now we do know that its adaptations are suited to all the wants of every one of its inhabitants—to the wants of the coral insect as well as to those of the whale. Hence we say *we know* that the sea has its system of circulation, for it transports materials for the coral rock from one part of the world to another; its currents receive them from the rivers, and hand them over to the little mason for the structure of the most stupendous works of solid masonry that man has ever seen—the coral islands of the sea".

The contemporary reviews of Maury's "Physical Geography of the Sea" gave unqualified praise to his style. The *Revue des Deux Mondes* declared, "Often indeed his powerful imagination makes of Maury a veritable poet, and his descriptions recall involuntarily those stories of the 'Thousand and One Nights', which charmed our childhood, where Gulnare pictures for her husband marvellously the mysterious realms of the profundities under the sea". Humboldt considered it an epoch-making book, and the French scientist Jomard congratulated Maury upon the accomplishment of a "work so difficult, so useful, so laborious", which he regarded as a true present to physicists, geographers, and navigators as well as to the commerce of all nations. The *Blackwood's Edinburgh Magazine* joined in the hymn of praise with the opinion that "the good that Maury has done, in awakening the powers of observation of the officers of the Royal and mercantile navies of England and America is incalculable", and added that such researches were exercising the most beneficial effect in improving and elevating the minds of seamen everywhere.

Some of Maury's theories, however, were early questioned, especially the one regarding the causes of ocean currents such as the Gulf Stream. He contended that they were set in motion by differences in specific gravity of the water in different places as caused by a disparity in temperature or in saltness. Sir John Herschel had considered that the currents were due entirely to the

Trade Winds; and C. Wyville Thomson, who thought that Maury's theory was ambiguous, was an adherent to the Herschel theory, though his colleague Carpenter was of a different opinion still.   "It is now known, however," writes Sir Willam A. Herdman,[1] "that the Gulf Stream is not an independent phenomenon, but is a part of the general system of surface circulation of the ocean, a system in which the currents, diverted to the east, as a result of the rotation of the earth in their course northwards from the equator, flow clockwise in the North Atlantic around a central, relatively calm area, the Sargasso Sea, in which seaweeds and other floating objects accumulate".

When one considers how science develops, one theory changing or giving place entirely to another as new and wider research is made, such criticisms as those above do not lessen at all the estimation of Maury's greatness as a pioneer scientist in a comparatively new field of investigation, nor do they at all rob him of the right to be called the world's first great oceanographer.   This is the opinion of a recent authority on the science of the sea, who writes, "Marine meteorology may be said to date from the time of M. F. Maury, U. S. Navy, whose 'Physical Geography of the Sea', though out of date as to facts and somewhat fantastic as to theories, remains a model book of popular science, written by a man who was possessed of all the knowledge of his time, and afire with the enthusiasm of research".[2]

Maury's researches in oceanography led to his con-

[1] "Founders of Oceanography", p. 175.

[2] From "Chapter I, The Air" by Hugh Robert Mill and D. Wilson Barker in *Science of the Sea*, edited by G. Herbert Fowler for the Challenger Society, 1912, p. 3.

nection with one of the most romantic and far-reaching scientific achievements of the century, the laying of the first Atlantic telegraph cable. Mention has already been made of the deep-sea soundings undertaken, under his direction, by American naval officers during the years 1849–1853. With the data furnished by these officers and by some others who were not engaged solely in sounding operations, Maury was enabled in the autumn of 1852 to construct an orographic map of the North Atlantic Ocean and to give a profile representing a vertical section of its bottom between America and Europe near the parallel of 39° north latitude. This showed the existence of what he called "the telegraphic plateau".

Up to this time no specimens of deep-sea ooze had been brought up from the bottom, and each sounding involved the loss of all the twine used as well as the cannon ball attached to it; and besides there was some uncertainty each time as to whether the bottom had really been reached. Fortunately, Lieutenant John Mercer Brooke, who was then at the Observatory, invented a simple but effective contrivance known as "Brooke's deep-sea sounding apparatus", which was well adapted to Maury's needs. The instrument was used by Lieutenant Berryman in the *Dolphin* during the year 1853 with great success, and the specimens which he obtained from the bottom were forwarded by Maury to Professor Bailey of West Point, for examination under the microscope. Upon examination the specimens were found not to contain a particle of sand or gravel mixed with them, but to be mites of sea-shells as perfect and unworn as when they were alive. This suggested to Maury the idea that there were no abrading forces at play upon the bottom of the deep sea, and that, if an electric cord were ever laid down upon the telegraphic plateau, there it would remain without anything to chafe or wear it except alone the tooth of time.

Accordingly, when in February, 1854 the projectors of the Atlantic Telegraph inquired of Maury as to the practicability of submerging the cable, he was able to reply as follows: "From Newfoundland to Ireland the distance between the nearest points is about sixteen hundred miles, and the bottom of the sea between the two places is a plateau, which seems to have been placed there especially for the purpose of holding the wires of a submarine telegraph and of keeping them out of harm's way. It is neither too deep nor too shallow; yet it is so deep that the wires, being once landed, will remain forever beyond the reach of vessels' anchors, icebergs, and drift of any kind, and so shallow that the wires may be readily lodged upon the bottom. The depth of this plateau is quite regular, gradually increasing from the shores of Newfoundland to the depth of from fifteen hundred to two thousand fathoms as you approach the other side. Whether it be better to lead the wires from Newfoundland or Labrador is not now the question; nor do I pretend to consider the question as to the possibility of finding a time calm enough, the sea smooth enough, a wire long enough, and a ship big enough to carry and lay a coil of wire 1600 miles in length. I simply address myself at this time to the question in so far as the bottom of the sea is concerned; and as for that, the greatest practical difficulty will, I apprehend, be found after reaching soundings at either end of the line, and not in the deep-sea. A wire laid across from either of the above-mentioned places on this side would pass to the north of the Grand Banks and rest on that beautiful plateau to which I have alluded, and where the water of the sea appears to be as quiet and as completely at rest as it is at the bottom of a mill-pond. Therefore, so far as the bottom of the deep-sea between Newfoundland or the mouth of the St. Lawrence and Ireland is concerned, the practicability of a submarine telegraph across the Atlantic is proved".

Maury first began in November, 1853 to correspond with Cyrus W. Field, one of the prime movers in the enterprise, and soon thereafter he met him personally. In the following year, Field invited Maury to become financially connected with the submarine telegraph, but this was declined on the grounds that he could not then be a disinterested adviser of the company. Field came to Maury often, sometimes every day for weeks at a time, to consult as to the size and material for the cable, which according to Field's first estimate was large enough, Maury playfully said, for the young whales to amuse themselves romping over it. Maury also devised a plan for making, coiling, and laying down the cable; and when somewhat later Field wrote asking on behalf of the company in regard to the best route and time for laying it, Maury with the help of his assistants consulted the results of 260,000 days of observations at sea and replied that the most propitious time for their undertaking would be either the last of July or the first of August, and that the steamer with the western end of the telegraphic cord on board would be less liable than the other to encounter a gale.

Field greatly appreciated Maury's advice, and invited him and his wife and two daughters to go on an excursion in the summer of 1855 to witness the laying of that part of the cable between Newfoundland and Cape Breton. He also gave permission that the National Observatory should be the first to use the telegraph to determine longitude across the Atlantic.   In giving this assurance, Field wrote of the great help which Maury was rendering in "illuminating the path for the lightning".

In the year 1856, Lieutenant Berryman in the *Arctic* made soundings from St. Johns, Newfoundland to Queenstown, Ireland, both on the outward and homeward passages.   But these soundings were very carelessly made, and finally had to be declared worthless by Maury.   In the summer of the following year Lieutenant Dayman, Royal Navy went over the same course in the *Cyclops* and made satisfactory soundings, which confirmed Maury's earlier statements as to the existence of the telegraphic plateau.

The company met with many discouragements in the laying of the cable.   An unsuccessful attempt was made in the summer of 1857, and three other failures followed the next year.   But perseverance finally had its reward; the U. S. Steamer *Niagara* and H. B. M. Steamer *Agamemnon*, after having met in mid-ocean and joined cables, set out for opposite shores where they arrived at Trinity Bay and Valentia Harbor, respectively, about the fifth of August, 1858.   There was great rejoicing on both sides of the Atlantic, and a great banquet was given in Field's honor by the city of New York at the Metropolitan Hotel on September 2, 1858.   In his address on that occasion, Field referred to the many to whom he was indebted and mentioned "those never-to-be-forgotten philosophers Lieutenant Maury, Professor

Morse, Professor Faraday, Professor Bache, and Professor W. Thomson, who have rendered more efficient aid without receiving any compensation".[3]

In October of the same year, the telegraph ceased to operate because of faulty insulation. It appears that the company had not carefully followed Maury's advice as to the size of the cable, and he had not himself been sanguine of success. After the failure, he contended that all that was needed was a cable heavy enough to sink with its own weight, and that there was no need for the iron wire which was wound round the gutta-percha that would itself be impervious to decay, that the strain of weight was all on the inner core of copper and had thus caused the trouble, that the iron wire on the outside might have interfered with the electric current, and that one large conducting wire instead of the seven threads woven together would have been better. But he added that he had no doubt as to the ultimate success of a telegraph across the Atlantic. Because of the Civil War, however, this was not to be accomplished until July, 1866; and as will be seen later, circumstances were then such as to prevent Maury from having any part in the final successful culmination of the project to which he had given so much thought and valuable assistance.

Maury's researches in the science of the sea could not, perhaps, have been so fruitful in practical achievements, had there not been at this time such a widespread desire to learn more about the ocean. In America, it was a veritable age of geographical investigation and dis-

---

[3] There is a tradition that Field said in this speech: "I am a man of few words: Maury furnished the brains, England gave the money, and I did the work." But diligent search has failed to discover any authority for the statement.

covery. In addition to the Exploring Expedition under Wilkes, which spent three years and ten months in exploring the islands of the Pacific and established the fact of the existence of the Antarctic continent, there were many others of the same nature. Lieutenant William Francis Lynch, in 1847–1848, led an expedition which surveyed the Dead Sea; in 1850–1851, Lieutenant Edward J. De Haven commanded a squadron which went into the Arctic in search of Sir John Franklin, and though unsuccessful in finding the English explorer, he made important scientific discoveries; Commander Cadwalader Ringgold, during 1853–1854, and then Commander John Rodgers, in the following years 1855–1856, explored and surveyed Bering Strait, the North Pacific Ocean, and the China Seas; and in 1853, Dr. Elisha K. Kane, U. S. Navy led another expedition into the Arctic regions in search of Franklin and off Greenland reached a stretch of water which he thought confirmed Maury's theory as to an open polar sea. Between 1848 and 1852, Lieutenant John P. Gilliss conducted an astronomical expedition to Chile, Lieutenant Archibald McRae traversed the Pampas from Chile to Buenos Ayres, Lieutenant Isaac G. Strain explored the Isthmus of Darien, Lieutenant Richard L. Page investigated the La Plata and its tributaries, and Lieutenant William Lewis Herndon made his famous trip across South America from the west coast to the headwaters of the Amazon and then down that stream to the Atlantic. Furthermore, it was at about this same time that Commodore Matthew Calbraith Perry went to Japan and by skillful diplomacy opened up that country to western civilization.

Maury simply reveled in the results of these various

explorations, and his writings are filled with references to them. He knew all the explorers personally, and furnished many of them with helpful advice and encouragement in their undertakings,—especially Kane, De Haven, Lynch, and Herndon. Dr. Kane wished to name the open polar sea after Maury; but he waived the honor and wrote to Kane that he should yield to his friends and let "his name go upon the waters", and to-day it is known as Kane Basin.

Maury's investigations into the habits and nature of whales had led him to conclude that there was really a Northwest Passage as well as open water about the North Pole. The former theory was proved by Commander McClure of H. M. S. *Investigator*, July 31, 1850 to April 6, 1853, when he passed from west to east through the northern waters, and settled the question. As to the polar sea, it is interesting to note in passing that only recently two explorers of the air, Byrd and Amundson, both verified the truth of Maury's theory.

As regards the Antarctic regions, Maury called upon the nations of the world to coöperate in sending an expedition there. "Ho for the South Pole" was his slogan. "It is enough for me", he wrote, "when contemplating the vast extent of that unknown region, to know that it is a part of the surface of our planet, and to remember that *the earth was made for man;* that all knowledge is profitable; that no discoveries have conferred more honor and glory upon the age in which they were made, or been more beneficial to the world than geographical discoveries; and that never were nations so well prepared to undertake Antarctic exploration as are those that I now solicit". Though the Civil War interfered with the carrying out of plans for the exploring of that portion of the globe, yet Maury's name deserves to be remembered among those whose continued interest in this enterprise finally led to the conquering of the South Pole.

Another contribution which Maury made was the laying down of lanes for steamers in the North Atlantic. The idea originated with R. B. Forbes of Boston, but was worked out scientifically by Maury. In the year 1855, at the instigation of a board of underwriters of New York, who paid for its cost, he published a chart illustrating what he called Ocean Lanes. To prepare this chart he studied the logs of 46,000 days of observations of the wind and weather of that part of the North Atlantic. Two tracks, or lanes, twenty miles wide, were laid down, to the more northern of which he proposed to confine the steamers westward bound, while the eastward bound vessels were to use the other, situated from one to ten degrees further south. Although the Secretary of the Navy immediately ordered the ships of the navy to observe these lanes, they were not generally adopted by the shipping of the world until about thirty-six years after they were formulated, and it was not until 1898 that all of the transatlantic steamship companies consented in a written agreement to use them. After a dispassionate investigation of the lanes, they said that they were impressed with the patience and researches that Maury must have made to have laid down such excellent paths, and they recognized that, had the highways been followed earlier, the great majority of the accidents which had befallen vessels in the North Atlantic might have been avoided.

Maury, then, was not merely a theorizer without the power of applying his ideas to the practical needs of men.

His greatness consisted in his being a man of vision and imagination, and at the same time a man of tremendous industry who was willing to toil endlessly that his theories might be made practical realities. This aim of unselfish service to humanity was displayed in all his researches in the science of the sea, from which came the works upon which his claim to fame chiefly rests. These were "The Wind and Current Charts", "Sailing Directions", and "The Physical Geography of the Sea". That such a claim is no idle one is borne out by the works themselves as well as by their influence upon all succeeding marine research, and it was the realization of this fact that led the Secretary of the Navy recently to give to the oceanographic research now being planned the name "Maury United States Naval Oceanographic Research".

SET OF SILVER MEDALS PRESENTED TO MAURY BY POPE PIUS IX

See page 65

Courtesy of "The Journal of American History," Vol. IV, Number 3 (1910).

MEDALS BESTOWED UPON MAURY

Gold medals bestowed upon Maury by the rulers of Sweden, Prussia, Holland, Austria, Sardinia, and France, the Republic of Bremen, and the Paris Universal Exhibition of 1855. See page 65.

CHAPTER VII

His Extra-Professional Interests

During the many years he spent at the Naval Observatory, Maury was by no means a narrow-minded specialist, as can be readily seen by a consideration of the wide range of his interests, which extended from the planting of sunflowers to keep malaria away from the Observatory to speculations as to the navigation of the air and a curious machine that was a kind of combination of phonograph and telephone. Before going forward with the story of his life, it would be well, therefore, to pause and consider some of these extra-professional activities that he was interested in.

Maury's interest in land meteorology had some connection, indeed, with his particular field of research; and in the beginning this was a part of his plan for a universal system of meteorological observations. But the opposition of Great Britain led him to withdraw it from the program of matters to be considered at the Brussels Conference, under the impression that a half of a loaf was better than no loaf at all. Upon his return to America after the conference, he began almost immediately to advocate the calling of another conference to consider land meteorology. As to the connection between the meteorology of the land and the sea he wrote in his "Sailing Directions" of 1855, "The great atmospherical ocean, at the bottom of which we are creeping along, and the laws of which touch so nearly the well-being of the whole human family, embraces the land as well as the sea, and neither those laws nor the movement and phenomena of the atmosphere can be properly studied or thoroughly investigated until observations, both by land and sea, shall enable us to treat the atmosphere as a whole".

The lukewarmness of Great Britain toward such a conference, and the Crimean War into which both that country and France entered, interfered with its meeting. But Maury continued to advocate a universal system of meteorological observations for the United States. He declared that it would cost no more to extend the system to the land than it had cost to spread it over the sea, and that, should it at any time be judged expedient so to enlarge the field of his researches as to include agriculture as well as commercial meteorology, he was ready at the bidding of the Department to submit a detailed plan for its consideration. The first fruits of his system of observations, which would be reported daily by telegraph and announced in the newspapers, would be, he said, that the farmers, merchants, and public in general would know with something like certainty the kind of weather to be expected, one, two, or more days in advance.

Maury addressed the United States Agricultural Society on the subject in Washington on January 10, 1856; and the question having been carried to the Agricultural Committee of the Senate, a bill was drawn in April to appropriate $20,000 to establish a system of daily observations. In June, Maury thought that Congress was disposed to enlarge on the idea and establish an Agricultural Bureau, but in August he wrote sadly that political events of a different nature had turned public attention away from meteorology and the advancement of science and directed the legislation of Congress to other subjects.

The bill was still pending, however, in the Senate early in 1857, and the details of Maury's plan were presented in Senator Harlan's report, made on behalf of the Committee on Agriculture. The following extract from this report will indicate to what extent those who afterwards established the United States Weather Bureau were indebted to Maury's plan: "It is believed that the Superintendent of the Observatory can obtain the necessary coöperation to enable him to subject the atmosphere to this system of research by an appeal to the farmers similar to that made to the mariners, if the Government will furnish appropriate instruments and defray the expense of transmitting this intelligence to the Hydrographical Office. In order that these observations might be reliable, the instruments with which they are to be made must be correct. An appropriation of a small sum of money would be necessary for the purchase of a few standard sets, to be distributed among the states and territories, for use and comparison, under suitable regulation to be prescribed by the Secretary of the Navy. It would be highly desirable, also, to be able to receive from all parts of the country daily reports by telegraph. In this way, the condition of the atmosphere in every part of the country, the presence of a storm in any quarter, its direction, its force, and the rapidity of its march could be known at every point any hour of the day; simultaneous reports from the various stations of the character of the weather, being received and combined at the central office, could not fail to afford results of the highest interest and advantage to every industrial pursuit. Storms, having their origin in one part of the world and taking up their line of march for another, may be thus narrowly watched by the mariner in communication with the land, in many instances for days before they would reach his shipping. Being forewarned, he could adopt the necessary means to evade their fury. The same intelligence thus communicated to the farmer and out-door laborer would be equally useful in its results. Every intelligent farmer, who is willing to note his observations, would become a sentinel on the watch-tower to admonish his fellow-laborers in the fields, as well as his co-laborers on the sea engaged in carrying his produce to distant markets, of approaching foul weather and consequent danger; and it is confidently maintained by those whose opinions are entitled to the greatest weight that with such a system of observation the laws that govern the course of those storms would soon be so well known that, in most cases, shipmasters and out-door laborers could be forewarned of their approach. Lieutenant Maury has also suggested that by mapping the skies, for example, of the United States, and adopting a system of signs and symbols, these telegraphic observations may be so projected on this map as to convey to the observer at a glance a knowledge of the appearance of the sky all over the whole country any hour in the day; and that by this means the change of the appearance of the sky, and subsequent changes of weather all over a continent, may be seen and studied from day to day; from which it is believed that science would deduce results of the highest importance. . . . . It has been suggested by Lieutenant Maury, and approved by your memorialists that the number of observers may be multiplied indefinitely by inviting the farmers, like the mariners at sea, to make voluntary observations of the weather, crops, soil, and flora, and report regularly to a common superintendent, by whom they also shall be discussed and classified".

This bill failed to become a law, and Maury's ambitious but reasonable plan for a system of land meteorology came to grief. The defeat of the measure was brought about largely through the opposition of Professor Henry, Secretary of the Smithsonian Institute, who considered that Maury's plan would be a rival to that proposed by him for the Smithsonian. Maury bitterly regretted this opposition, and in an address delivered in October, 1859 before the North Alabama Agricultural and Mechanical Association at Decatur he said, "Some years ago I proposed, you recollect, a system of agricultural meteorology for farmers, and of daily weather reports by telegraph from all parts of the country for the benefit of mankind. The Smithsonian Institution and the Agricultural Bureau of the Patent Office stole this idea and attempted to carry it out, but with what success let silence tell. Take notice now that this plan of crop reports is 'my thunder', and if you see some one in Washington running away with it there, recollect if you please where the lightning came from".

Maury continued to agitate this question by both letters and public addresses particularly among the people of the Great Lakes region and of the South, until the outbreak of the Civil War. This put an end for the time being to Maury's attempts to establish a system of land meteorology in the United States and to his endeavors to bring together another international conference at which a scheme could be devised for making universal land and sea meteorological observations.

But after the war was over, he returned to the question, as will be noted later, with his characteristic persistence and energy.

In 1848 Maury's mind was intent on the shortening of communications by sea, and out of that problem grew his interest in the first trans-continental railroad. His opinion at first was that the most direct route to China would be by rail from Memphis to Monterey on the Pacific, and thence by great circle sailing by way of the Fox Islands which were convenient for coaling stations. He enthusiastically wrote that, if there were a canal already cut from Chagres to Panama, the circuity of the route and the loss of time compared with what was to be gained by the proposed line from Memphis to Monterey would in time cause the abandonment of the former and the completion of the latter. Meanwhile the gold rush to California had begun, and Maury then decided that both a railroad across the continent and a canal, or railroad, across the Isthmus of Panama should be constructed. As president of the Memphis Convention of representatives from fourteen states, which met October 23, 1849, he urged both projects, and eventually each of the two routes was made available as a highway of transportation between the East and the West.

In connection with Maury's advocacy of the Isthmian route, there was a story told by his nephew which throws light upon his uncle's sterling character. It appeared that some papers of his upon the advantages of a route to the East by way of the Isthmus attracted much attention, and a Northern firm wrote him a letter, enclosing a check for $500 in token of approbation of his views which strongly promoted the interests of their business. He was asked to continue his advocacy of that route, and was assured that the enclosure was but a mere earnest of what they would pay for his continued support. "Please to look at this", Maury said; "these people seem to think money the chief object of all endeavor". He returned the check then with a courteous note of thanks explaining that he could not admit personal interest into his discussions of measures for the general good of the people.

Another question of great importance, to which Maury gave his voice and pen for many years, was the financial and maritime interests of the South and West. As early as January, 1839, he wrote an article for the *Southern Literary Messenger* on "Direct Trade with the South", in which he called upon the people of that section to establish a line of steam packets between Norfolk and Havre. In the year 1845, he wrote for the same magazine his "Letters to Clay", in which he advocated the establishment of a dockyard, a school for apprentices, and a naval academy at Memphis, the construction of a canal from the upper Mississippi to the Lakes, the establishment of a naval base at Pensacola as well as at some other point on the Atlantic coast south of Norfolk, and the placing of fortifications at Key West and the Dry Tortugas for the protection of the Gulf. These measures he continued to advocate in season and out of season.

After Congress passed on June 15, 1844, an act for establishing a naval dockyard and depot at Memphis, Maury concentrated his batteries upon the need for a canal to connect the Mississippi with Lake Michigan through the Illinois River. He claimed that this would be of great benefit to commerce in time of peace, and that, if war with England should come, the United

States would then be prepared to meet her halfway. "Let this work be completed", he added, "and it will be a dragon's tooth planted in the West to bring forth for the defense of the country a harvest of steam-clad warriors, ever brave, always ready".

This question he took up again at the meeting of the Memphis Convention of Southern and Western States, on November 12, 1845, where he was the veritable spokesman of those two sections. Another important matter which he advocated at this convention was what was called "A Warehousing System and Direct Trade with the South". This, he said, would foster shipping for Southern ports, enable ships to be loaded both ways and thus make cheaper rates, and prevent trade in high-dutied articles from concentrating in New York where there was the greatest amount of ready capital on hand. Other measures which Maury urged at this convention were the following: bakeries at Chicago for supplying better bread for the navy, a school of engineers at Memphis, mail and snag-boats as a nucleus for a river fleet in time of war, river marks or gauges as an aid to safer navigation, the deepening of the river below New Orleans at Southwest Pass, more lighthouses on the Florida and the Gulf Coast, and a monthly mail to Oregon.

In 1851, at the request of the Secretary of the Navy, Maury wrote a report on "Fortifications" to be referred to the House Committee on Military Affairs. In this report he advocated for coast defense what he called "a locomotive battery or flying artillery" to protect cities from the "Great Guns of Big Ships"; heavy fortifications at Key West, on the Dry Tortugas, and perhaps on Ship and Cat Islands; and the completion of railroad connection with the Pacific and the beginning there of the nucleus of a navy. He was opposed to floating batteries, but favored twenty or twenty-five steam men-of-war as a home squadron and thought some provision should be made against surprise on the Lakes. In closing, he declared, "The ocean front of the United States alone is greater in extent than the ocean front of the whole of Europe; therefore, like action to the orator, a navy to us is the first, second, and third chief requisite to any effective system of national defense".

The same year Maury turned again to the "Commercial Prospects of the South", which he made the subject of an address before the Virginia Mercantile Convention at Richmond. In this he called attention to what might have happened if Norfolk had become the terminus of a French line of steam packets to Havre, as he had suggested some dozen years before. Now, he said, the South must look toward the south; in view of the importance of "our Mediterranean" into which big rivers flow that are the arteries of much commerce, and because of the potential riches of the Amazon which will be vastly increased by the construction of a canal or railroad across the Isthmus, a line of steamers from Norfolk, Charleston, or Savannah to the mouth of the Amazon should at once be established. This enterprise, together with the need for building railroads in the South, was constantly in Maury's mind and often became a subject of correspondence down to the beginning of the Civil War.

Maury seems to have become almost as ready a speaker as he was a writer, and as his fame grew he was frequently called upon to speak on scientific questions and large problems of a commercial nature. In 1846, he addressed the Philodemic Society at the commencement exercises of Georgetown College in Washington. In the course of his speech he lauded the study of science in this fashion: "Beauties far more lovely, poetry far more sublime, lessons inexpressibly more eloquent and instructive than any which the classic lore of ancient Greece or Rome ever afforded are now to be seen and gathered in the walks of science". In 1855 he spoke to the Jefferson and Washington Literary Societies of the University of Virginia, beginning with what he referred to as "sailing directions". "There are some here", he declared, "who though not seamen are nevertheless about to become masters of their own acts, and who are about to try the voyage of life upon a troubled sea. I have been some little time on that voyage; and it is so that, whenever I see a young man relying upon his own resources and setting out alone upon this long voyage, my heart warms towards him. I always desire to range up alongside of him, to speak to him kindly, and whisper words of encouragement in his ear".

Then he told the young men that they should have ambition to do even better than their fathers had done; that they should not lose sight of the welfare of the community and the prosperity of the commonwealth; and that they should give Virginia again her place of leadership among the states, and take away from the South the allegation that she is wanting in enterprise. He closed with the following rules of conduct: "Whatever may be the degree of success that I have met with in life, I attribute it, in a great measure, to the adoption of such rules. One was never to let the mind be idle for want of useful occupation, but always to have in reserve subjects of thought or study for the leisure moments and quiet hours of the night. When you read

a book, let it be with the view to special information.
The habits of mind to be thus attained are good, and the
information useful.   It is surprising how difficult one
who attempts this rule finds it at first to provide himself
with subjects for thought—to think of something that he
does not know.   In our ignorance our horizon is very
contracted: mists, clouds, and darkness hang upon it,
and self fills almost the entire view around, above, and
below to the utmost verge.   But as we study the laws of
nature, and begin to understand about our own ignorance, we find light breaking through, the horizon ex-
panding, and self getting smaller and smaller.   It is
like climbing a mountain: every fact or fresh discovery
is a step upward with an enlargement of the view, until
the unknown and the mysterious become boundless
—self infinitely small; and the conviction comes upon us
with a mighty force that we know nothing—that human
knowledge is only a longing desire."   In conclusion, he
warned them against believing that they had finished
their education on leaving the University, for they had
merely cleared away the rubbish and prepared the foundations.   If they ceased to study, they soon would forget
what they had learned and mental retrogression would
begin; for just as movement and progress were necessary
aspects of life in the physical world so were rest and
decay correlative terms in the mental and moral realms.

Among the numerous addresses which he delivered
during the decade preceding the Civil War, the most
eloquent and significant was the one given on October
10, 1860, at the laying of the corner stone of the University of the South at Sewanee, Tennessee.   For this
occasion there were assembled eight bishops, two hundred presbyters, and five thousand people.   In intro-

ducing Maury, Bishop Otey, his old teacher and friend, referred to him as a distinguished fellow-citizen, whose labors in the cause of science have crowned his name with honor throughout the world and made him, in a manner, the property of all the nations, for the winds of Heaven and the waves of the sea had been made tributary by him to increasing the facilities of trade to every land and on every sea where commerce spreads her sails.

Maury's address, which is quoted in its entirety as an example of his oratorical power, was as follows: "Ladies and Gentlemen: This greeting and the terms in which my old preceptor and early friend has brought me into this presence fill me with emotions difficult to utter. I thank you for your goodness.

"Physical geography makes the whole world kin. Of all the departments in the domains of physical science, it is the most Christianizing. Astronomy is grand and sublime; but astronomy overpowers with its infinities, overwhelms with its immensities. Physical geography charms with its wonders, and delights with the benignity of its economy. Astronomy ignores the existence of man; physical geography confesses that existence, and is based on the Biblical doctrine that the earth was made for man. Upon no other theory can it be studied; upon no other theory can its phenomena be reconciled. The astronomer computes an ephemeris for his comets; predicts their return; tells the masses of the planets, and measures by figures the distance of the stars. But whether stars, planets, or comets be peopled or not is in his arguments, theories, and calculations of no consequence whatever. He regards the light and heat of the sun as emanations—forces to guide the planets in their orbits, and light comets in their flight—nothing more. But the physical geographer, when he warms himself by the coal fire in winter, or studies by the light of the gas burner at night, recognizes in the light and heat which he then enjoys the identical light and heat which ages ago came from the sun, and which with provident care and hands benignant have been bottled away in the shape of a mineral and stored in the bowels of the earth for man's use, thence to be taken at his convenience, and liberated at will for his manifold purposes.

"Here, in the schools which are soon to be opened, within the walls of this institution which we are preparing to establish in this wood, and the corner stone of which has just been laid, the masters of this newly ordained science will teach our sons to regard some of the commonest things as the most important agents in the physical economy of our planet.   They are also mighty ministers of the Creator.   Take this water" (holding up a glassful) "and ask the student of physical geography to explain a portion only of its multitudinous offices in helping to make the earth fit for man's habitation.   He may recognize in it a drop of the very same which watered the Garden of Eden when Adam was there.   Escaping thence through the veins of the earth into the rivers, it reached the sea; passing along its channels of circulation, it was conveyed far away by its currents to those springs in the ocean which feed the winds with vapor for rains among these mountains; taking up the heat in these southern climes, where otherwise it would become excessive, it bottles it away in its own little vesicles. These are invisible; but rendering the heat latent and innocuous, they pass like sightless couriers of the air through their appointed channels, and arrive here in the upper sky. This mountain draws the heat from them; they are formed into clouds and condensed into rain, which, coming to the earth, make it 'soft with showers', causing the trees of the field to clap their hands, the valleys to shout, and the mountains to sing. Thus the earth is made to yield her increase, and the heart of man is glad.

"Nor does the office of this cup of water in the physical economy end here. It has brought heat from the sea in the southern hemisphere to be set free here for the regulation of our climates; it has ministered to the green plants, and given meat and drink to man and beast. It has now to cater among the rocks for the fish and insects of the sea. Eating away your mountains, it fills up the valleys, and then, loaded with lime and salts of various minerals, it goes singing and dancing and leaping back to the sea, owning man by the way as a taskmaster—turning mills, driving machinery, transporting merchandise for him—and finally reaching the ocean. It there joins the currents to be conveyed to its appointed place, which it never fails to reach in due time, with food in due quantities for the inhabitants of the deep, and with materials of the right kind to be elaborated in the workshops of the sea into pearls, corals, and islands—all for man's use.

"Thus the right-minded student of this science is brought to recognize in the dewdrop the materials of which He who 'walketh upon the wings of the wind' maketh His chariot. He also discovers in the raindrop a clue by which the Christian philosopher may be conducted into the very chambers from which the hills are watered.

"I have been blamed by men of science, both in this

country and in England, for quoting the Bible in confirmation of the doctrines of physical geography. The Bible, they say, was not written for scientific purposes, and is therefore of no authority in matters of science. I beg pardon! The Bible *is* authority for everything it touches. What would you think of the historian who should refuse to consult the historical records of the Bible, because the Bible was not written for the purposes of history? The Bible is true and science is true. The agents concerned in the physical economy of our planet are ministers of His who made both it and the Bible. The records which He has chosen to make through the agency of these ministers of His upon the crust of the earth are as true as the records which, by the hands of His prophets and servants, He has been pleased to make in the Book of Life. They are both true; and when your men of science, with vain and hasty conceit, announce the discovery of disagreement between them, rely upon it the fault is not with the Witness or His records, but with the 'worm' who essays to interpret evidence which he does not understand.

"When I, a pioneer in one department of this beautiful science, discover the truths of revelation and the truths of science reflecting light one upon the other and each sustaining the other, how can I, as a truth-loving, knowledge-seeking man, fail to point out the beauty and to rejoice in its discovery? Reticence on such an occasion would be sin, and were I to suppress the emotion with which such discoveries ought to stir the soul, the waves of the sea would lift up their voice, and the very stones of the earth cry out against me. (Great applause.)

"As a student of physical geography, I regard the

earth, sea, air, and water, as parts of a machine, pieces of mechanism not made with hands, but to which nevertheless certain offices have been assigned in the terrestrial economy. It is good and profitable to seek to find out these offices, and point them out to our fellows; and when, after patient research, I am led to the discovery of any one of them, I feel with the astronomer of old as though I had 'thought one of God's thoughts'—and tremble. Thus as we progress with our science we are permitted now and then to point out here and there in the physical machinery of the earth a design of the Great Architect when He planned it all.

"Take the little nautili. Where do the fragile creatures go? What directing hand guides them from sea to sea? What breeze fills the violet sails of their frail little craft, and by whose skill is it enabled to brave the sea and defy the fury of the gale? What mysterious compass directs the flotilla of these delicate and graceful argonauts? Coming down from the Indian Ocean, and arriving off the stormy cape, they separate—the one part steering for the Pacific, the other for the Atlantic Ocean. Soon the ephemeral life that animates these tiny navigators will be extinct; but the same power which cared for them in life now guides them in death, for though dead their task in the physical economy of our planet is not finished, nor have they ceased to afford instruction in philosophy. The frail shell is now to be drawn to distant seas by the lower currents. Like the leaf carried through the air by the wind, the lifeless remains descend from depth to depth by an insensible fall even to the appointed burial place on the bottom of the deep; there to be collected into heaps and gathered into beds which at some day are to appear above the surface a storehouse rich with fertilizing ingredients for man's use. Some day science will sound the depth to which this dead shell has fallen, and the little creature will perhaps afford solution for a problem a long time unsolved; for it may be the means of revealing the existence of the submarine currents that have carried it off, and of enabling the physical geographer to trace out the secret paths of the sea. (Great applause).

"Had I time, I might show how mountains, deserts, winds, and water, when treated by this beautiful science, all join in one universal harmony—for each one has its part to perform in the great concert of nature. (Renewed applause).

"The Church, ere physical geography had yet attained to the dignity of a science in our schools, and even before man had endowed it with a name, saw and appreciated its dignity,—the virtue of its chief agents. What have we heard chanted here in this grove by a thousand voices this morning?—A song of praise, such as these hills have not heard since the morning stars sang together:—the Benedicite of our Mother Church, invoking the very agents whose workings and offices it is the business of the physical geographer to study and point out! In her services she teaches her children in their songs of praise to call upon certain physical agents, *principals*, in this newly established department of human knowledge,—upon the waters above the firmament; upon showers and dew; wind, fire, and heat; winter and summer; frost and cold; ice and snow; night and day; light and darkness; lightning and clouds; mountains and hills; green things, trees, and plants;

whales, and all things that move in the waters; fowls of the air, with beasts and cattle,—to bless, praise, and magnify the Lord. (Tremendous applause.)

"To reveal to man the offices of these agents in making the earth his fit dwelling place is the object of physical geography. Said I not well that of all the sciences physical geography is the most Christianizing in its influences?" (Long continued applause.)

In addition to his occasional speeches, Maury also appeared on the regular lecture platform, where he delivered three different series of lectures. "My lot in life", he wrote, "is cast among those whose necessities compel them to stop with philosophy now and then and 'court Dame Fortune's golden smile' until she vouchsafe a few extra centimes with which one may propitiate butcher and baker. Yielding to these necessities, I have occasionally to abandon the winds and the sea, and go digging in the hopes of finding a few of the 'roots of evil' wherewith to propitiate amiable creditors. These necessities have been pressing upon me, so I had to abandon everything and go out on a lecturing tour". In this connection, it is of interest to note that in addition to his salary of $3,500 as Superintendent of the Observatory Maury received from Harper's as royalties on his "Physical Geography of the Sea" from $300 to $400 a year up to the Civil War. He was also paid considerable sums for his contributions to the magazines, such as the *Southern Literary Messenger*, from which according to his account book he received over $600 from November, 1841 to December, 1842. Maury had, however, a large family of eight children, and their needs increased from year to year.

His first series of regular lectures, six in number, was

delivered before the Lowell Institute of Boston in December, 1856, on the general subject of "The Winds and Currents of the Sea". The Boston *Daily Evening Transcript* reported the lectures and gave great praise to "Professor" Maury; while one who heard him wrote in a personal letter, "It was a truly interesting lecture and from our citizens there comes forth one response, *Excellent, Capital, The Lecture of the Season.* It was no common audience, I assure you. Many were present who seldom attend evening lectures. All were enthusiastic in their praise. I was told by men high in office and the estimation of the community that it was the best lecture and the most interesting to them that they had ever heard. It was Lyceum night and the hour of commencement was postponed in order tó give that audience a chance to hear, and they came and heard; notwithstanding they had been sitting an hour to another lecture, they sat still one and one-quarter hours more and so still that throughout the whole one might have heard a pin drop".

For these lectures Maury was paid the sum of $500; and on the same tour he delivered ten other lectures in Massachusetts and New York at $50 a lecture. In New York he spoke at Albany, Rochester, Syracuse, and Buffalo. In the last-mentioned city two lectures were given on November 27 and 28, and the account of the first of these in the Buffalo *Commercial Advertiser* is most interesting. "We listened to Lieutenant Maury", it reports, "with unalloyed pleasure. His appearance is that of a kind-hearted, benevolent man of fifty; his forehead that of a philosopher, his eyes and lower face indicative of poetic sentiment. His delivery is neither good nor bad, but he found no difficulty in enchaining the attention of his audience, and few, we presume, cared much for the lack of oratorical effect. We had never given Lieutenant Maury credit for the power of poetical description which he manifested in this lecture. Beautifully written, rich in descriptive power and full of a sailor's love for his ship, and his fondness for strange scenes, we have rarely listened to a better specimen of 'word painting' than that which referred to a western passage across the Pacific. But immediately after came a description of the climate of Valparaiso, equally vivid, and in his allusion to the stars of the Southern hemisphere even more eloquent—one saw that night sky, a vault of steel, the brilliant stars which shone upon its surface and the planets brighter still, seemingly swimming in mid air beneath them; and the Magellan clouds, 'rents in the azure robe of night, through which one looked into the black profound of space beyond' ".

On his next lecture tour, during November and December, 1858, Maury was gone about a month; he traveled some five thousand miles and delivered twenty-five lectures, at the following places: Rochester, Buffalo, Cleveland, Ann Arbor, Chicago, Detroit, Kalamazoo, Indianapolis, Laporte, Cincinnati, Springfield, and St. Louis. The subjects that he discussed were: The Atlantic Telegraph, The Highways and Byways of the Sea, On Extending to the Lakes a System of Meteorological Observations for the Benefit of Lake Commerce and Navigation, On the Workshops and Harmonies of the Sea, and The Importance of a Careful Meteorological Survey of the Great North American Lakes.

The various newspapers of these cities reported large and appreciative audiences, with many often turned away for lack of seats; and they invariably praised the

lectures. For example, the Indianapolis *Daily Sentinel*
declared, "(The subject) was presented in such a pleasing
and attractive form, and the facts, the experiments, and
the analogies from which his conclusions were drawn
were stated so clearly and clothed so beautifully that it
seemed to the hearer rather like the fanciful description
of the poet than the details of experimental philosophy".
The Cleveland *Plain Dealer* thus expressed its praise:
"(His theme) was treated with a mastery of facts, an
array of historical data, and a thoroughness and com-
pleteness of detail and all with a clearness, vigor, and
force of language highly instructive and deeply and
powerfully interesting. Without any of the graces of
oratory, or the beauties and effects of elocution, without
even the charms of an agreeable delivery, Lieutenant
Maury invested his subject with a degree of interest and
power of attraction that was such as to challenge the
admiration and rivet the attention of his auditors from
the opening to the close". The tour was evidently a
great success, but the exposure to the wintry storms so
damaged Maury's health as to bring on an attack of
rheumatic gout on his return home, a disease from which
he continued to suffer off and on until his death fifteen
years later.

The following autumn, however, he was lecturing
again, this time in Alabama and Tennessee. While in
Nashville to address the State Agricultural Bureau, he
was invited by the Tennessee Historical Society to deliver in the Hall of the House of Representatives of the
Capitol his lecture on "The Geography of the Sea".
This was on October 12, 1859, and on the following day
Maury visited the House while in session and was welcomed by Speaker Whitthorne in the high-flown language

which was popular at that day, as one who "has by his genius and his talents made himself the peer of earth's great men, and who by his wooing of the stars has made them to give forth speech and by his control of the winds of the sea has compelled their obedience to man and made them to become ministers of his happiness".

All of this speaking and writing made Maury's name known very widely all over the United States, and it was but natural for some of his friends to think of him in connection with the Presidency. They believed that, if his adopted state, Tennessee, would heartily nominate him, not as a party man but as a broad-minded, public-spirited citizen, he could be easily elected, for his popularity was great with all who did not aspire to the leadership of some particular clique. But Maury did not like politics, and besides Fate had in store for him an entirely different future. However, in the light of his attitude toward slavery and the preservation of the Union it is interesting to speculate on how different the history of the United States might have been, had he been elevated to this high office.

MATTHEW FONTAINE MAURY

This painting, by E. Sophonisba Hergesheimer, was presènt in 1923 to the United States Naval Academy by the United Daughters of the Confederacy, Atlanta Chapter, Georgia Division. It hangs over the entrance to the Maury Hall wing of the Academic Group of buildings.

CHAPTER VIII

His Treatment by the "Retiring Board"

It must not be supposed that Maury spent only hal-
cyon days during his long period of service at the Naval
Observatory. When it is remembered that his contacts
with men were extremely numerous, and that the opportunities for unpleasant controversy were almost without
number in view of the fact that he was such an ardent
advocate of whatever question he took up, whether it
was scientific, economic, or political, it is truly remarkable that there were so few who became hostile to him.
But strange as it may seem, those who as a class were
most unfriendly to Maury and least sympathetic toward
his work were a considerable number of his brother
officers in the navy. As a consequence, in the year 1855,
a board of naval officers inflicted upon him painful
mental sufferings and placed him in a humiliating
position, at the very time when his name was being
acclaimed by the scientists and many of the rulers of
foreign countries.

The occasion for the display of this enmity against
Maury was the passing of the Act of Congress of February 28, 1855, to "promote the efficiency of the navy".
To carry out this law, the President assembled a board of
naval officers consisting of five captains, five commanders, and five lieutenants, to "make a careful examination" of the personnel of the navy and report those
found "incapable of performing promptly and efficiently
all their duty both ashore and afloat". Those so reported were to be either dropped from the rolls of the

navy or placed upon what was to be called the "reserved list" and receive either leave of absence pay or
furlough pay, according to the degree of their disability;
they were, moreover, to be ineligible for further promotion, and subject at all times to the Navy Department
for duty.

The members of this board were Captains William B.
Shubrick, Matthew C. Perry, Charles S. McCauley,
C. K. Stribling, and Abraham Bigelow; Commanders
G. J. Pendergrast, Franklin Buchanan, Samuel F. Du
Pont, and Andrew H. Foote; and Lieutenants John S.
Missroon, Richard L. Page, Sylvanus W. Godon, William
L. Maury, and James S. Biddle. The board met on the
20th of June, and continued its sessions daily, except
for Sundays and the 4th of July, until it finished its work
on July 25, and the following day it reported the results
of its deliberations. Its judgment was that seventy-one
officers should be placed on the "reserved on leave of
absence pay" list, and eighty-one on the "reserved on
furlough pay" list; while forty-nine were recommended
to be "dropped from the navy".

Official announcement of these results was not made
until some weeks later, and Maury did not receive
notice from the Secretary of the Navy until September
17, 1855 that his name had been placed on the "reserved
on leave of absence pay" list. The Secretary's letter,
however, informed him that he was not detached from
the Naval Observatory, but was to continue on his present duty.

To this letter Maury at once replied, "This announcement has taken me by surprise. I have been in the
navy upwards of thirty years. During this time I have
aimed in every station to which I have been called to

serve my country truly and well, with what success the Department and the public can judge better than I. Suffice it to say, that I am not aware that any charges or accusations or even any complaint of duty neglected or badly performed during this long period has ever reached the Department against me. Nevertheless in the judgment of the Board I should be and have been placed under official disgrace. This is a severe blow and I feel it as a grievous wrong. May I not therefore be permitted to know what is the accusation against me and who my accusers were before the Board?" The Secretary answered that the Board in accordance with the law simply gave names and ranks, and did not assign reasons for its decisions.

Maury felt that he had been made to suffer a grievous wrong, and began to appeal to his friends to help him to secure justice. He was particularly incensed over the fact that the Board met in secret, and that he could find out neither what his offense was nor who his accusers were. Some of the members of this "monstrous inquisition", he declared, had publicly condemned all science in the navy, and none of the Board except Perry had made any mark upon the service that would be recognized as a reminder of their excellence when they were gone. He could think of only two reasons for their action against him. In the first place, there was a spirit of jealousy that he, a mere lieutenant, had dared to establish a reputation somewhat honorable in spite of them; and in the second place, they would attempt to offer as an excuse for the slur they had cast upon him the fact that he was lame. As to the latter reason, Maury wrote, "Mere bodily activity, in an officer of my rank, is comparatively of little value, when taken in connection with the mental activity. Officers are expected—at least, it is generally so in the upper grades—to work rather with the head than the hand, and, moreover, I am bodily as active as a majority of the Board, and if broken legs disqualify, at least one member of the Board should have borne me company, for his leg was broken twice over. . . . General Scott is crippled in the arm, yet it does not appear to have unfitted him for the army. Besides, this Board has left untouched other crippled officers, both above and below me".

The action of the Board produced a very mischievous and demoralizing effect on the naval service, upon which it let loose the spirit of a hyena. Officers began to investigate the antecedents of each other, and all sorts of trouble-making scandal was unearthed. But fortunately for Maury nothing could be found prejudicial against his character and his record in the files of the Navy Department, and he exulted over the fact that he had never tripped in his youth. He became disgusted with all the accusations and insinuations that had been aroused, and declared that they were heartsickening to a man who loved to live at peace with all the world.

It was necessary, however, for him to see the matter through. So he again wrote to the Secretary of the Navy, complaining that he had been given no hearing, that all action had been taken in secret, no minutes or records of any kind having been kept, and that the charge of incompetency was too vague; and therefore he asked for specific charges and for a fair and open trial according to law. The Secretary replied that the members of the Board had dispersed to their duties; but that he would reassemble them if the President so directed, adding that Maury had a "spotless character and eminent service". Another interchange of letters took place, in which Maury said he could not see the action of the Board otherwise than as official disgrace to him; while the Secretary wrote that the President was of the opinion that the Board acted in accordance with the law and that there was no authority under it to command them to report the reasons for their recommendations.

Maury then decided to write a letter to each member of the Board and ask the following questions: "1st. What was the process of examination adopted by the Board for ascertaining whether an officer was efficient or not? 2nd. What was the standing of efficiency for the grade of lieutenant? 3rd. What difference, if any, did the Board make between duty ashore and duty afloat? 4th. Wherein was I found incapable of performing the duties of my office, rank, or grade? 5th. Did the Board inspect the Observatory, or make other examination as to the manner in which it is conducted? 6th. What was the character of the evidence upon which the Board pronounced its findings against me?"

All replies to these letters were unsatisfactorily evasive, but in general they agreed in considering that Maury had not been placed in official disgrace. Perry wrote, "In justice to those who have been affected by the action of the Board, I cannot but hope that steps may soon be taken by the proper authorities to develop the causes and explain the circumstances which have brought about this painful change in our common service". But the junior member, Biddle, wrote most fully, and gave the impression that he thought that the accident to Maury's leg had unfitted him for sea service and that on this ground he had voted for his retirement. He added that each officer should perform his part of the most unpleasant duty in the navy, service afloat, and he implied that he believed Maury had been unwilling to go to sea because of "love of scientific distinction".

Meanwhile the press of the country had taken up Maury's cause, and a few examples from the newspapers will show how high the feeling ran. The *Scientific American* wrote, "To use the language of the Philadelphia *Inquirer*, we regard the action of the Board 'as an insult upon the virtue and general intelligence of the country'. . . . (Maury's) eminent services have been acknowledged by almost every government in Europe. Prussia and Sweden have struck gold medals to his honor. The Russian Ambassador has publicly thanked him by the direction of his government. England has not been sparing of her tribute of admiration in Parliament, and has adopted his plans in her own navy, while the great French Industrial Exhibition awards to his charts her highest premiums. His own country, on the contrary, declares him a clog and an incumbrance on its navy, and unworthy of promotion. We trust Congress will set this matter right. Better dispense with the services of the entire Board of 'ten minutes inquisitors' than of this eminent man. We understand that it had been proposed in Philadelphia, in case Lieutenant Maury retired from the Observatory, to present him with a testimonial of $50,000, as an acknowledgment of his services, and as a mark of the disapprobation of the action of the Board. We doubt not that this sum might easily be raised in our great commercial cities. Yes, twice that if necessary".

The New York *Herald* held the Board up for ridicule, in the following fashion: "I understand there is now in press, and will shortly appear, a history of the lives and eminent services of the late Retiring Board, entitled 'Lights and Shadows of the Fifteen'. It will embrace all the shades in the lives of those fifteen Spartans, from their entrance into the service up to their 'Thermopylae defeat' of 201 brothers in arms, by which gallant action they 'promoted themselves'. It will be the commencement of a new epoch in the naval history of the country, and will be rich, racy, and spicy".

Further quotations from the New York *Journal of Commerce*, the *National Intelligencer*, and other newspapers might be given, in which the contention was made that, without respect to party, the sentiment was practically unanimous that Maury should be restored to his place on the active list with all the "honor and reparation due to injured merit", and that this should be done without further delay. But two more years were to pass before justice was done. Even after both the President and the Secretary of the Navy had come to realize that Maury had been unjustly treated, there was considerable further delay while Congress formulated a plan for undoing the action of the Board in cases where mistakes had been made. Petitions had been presented by Senators for about one hundred of the officers affected, and these occasioned endless debates in the halls of Congress during the year 1856. Senator Bell of Tennessee presented the petition on Maury's behalf before the Senate on January 21, 1856, and made several long speeches in its defense.

Senator Mallory of Florida, who had sponsored the bill for promoting efficiency in the navy, was naturally a strong defender of the action of the Board, and when Maury's petition was presented he said, among other things, "If the Board has erred in any case whatever,

there was no error in the case of Lieutenant Maury",
for he declared that his physical disability was sufficient
cause and he had repeatedly shunned sea service. There
seems to have been no personal animus in Mallory's
stand, which appears to have been merely the defense of
a party measure; indeed, only one year before, when it
was proposed in the Senate to make a remuneration of
$25,000 to Maury for the service to the country of his
wind and current charts, Mallory as chairman of the
Senate Committee on Naval Affairs made a long and
favorable report, in which he reviewed in detail Maury's
work and quoted words of praise from the reports of
Secretaries of the Navy Graham, Kennedy, and Dobbin.
His report concluded with these words: "This officer
has been for years in the public service, has a family to
provide for, and is entirely dependent upon his annual
pay; and for these reasons your Committee think that a
sum of money, insignificant indeed in comparison to his
services, yet sufficient to remove his anxieties and to
cheer his hopes for the future of those dependent upon
him, might be justly bestowed. Your Committee recommend that a sum of 25,000 dollars be thus appropriated, and report a bill accordingly". Such a sudden
turn from eloquent support of Maury to opposition to
his interests was indeed remarkable, for it was a long
jump from the advocacy of a measure awarding him
$25,000 to one which reduced his salary from $3,500 to
$1,200 a year. Mallory was supported in his defense
of the action of the Board, as it affected Maury, mainly
by Senators Clayton of Delaware, Benjamin of Louisiana, and Jefferson Davis of Mississippi.

Eventually, however, the Senate Committee on Naval
Affairs reported a bill to amend the act entitled "An Act

to Promote the Efficiency of the Navy", which was finally passed on January 16, 1857. This provided that an officer whose status in the navy had been affected by the action of the Retiring Board could by written request secure an investigation, by regular court of inquiry, into his "physical, mental, professional, and moral fitness" for the naval service, and that the finding of this court might be submitted to the President, who was to take action accordingly.

The bill originally contained two additional sections, providing for the establishment of the rank of admiral and the organization of a scientific corps in the navy; but they were finally struck out. This scientific corps was to take charge of the Naval Observatory, the nautical almanac, the hydrographical work, and such other scientific matters as the Secretary of the Navy should prescribe; and its personnel was to consist of one captain, two commanders, ten lieutenants, and seven masters. Mallory favored the establishment of such a plan, and, about-facing again, said on the floor of the Senate, "The Committee had an earnest desire that that distinguished officer (Maury) should be at the head of the corps". Though Maury had written at first rather enthusiastically of the scientific corps, he eventually came to the conclusion that it would not have been wise to establish it, and wrote that he was not sorry it had been struck out of the bill.

Under the main provisions of the amended act, Maury's case was taken up by a court of inquiry, before whom it was proved by a surgeon that his leg was actually stronger than that of Missroon, one of the members of the Board; that he had not tried to evade sea service but had applied for such service during the

Mexican War and had been refused; that other officers retained on the active list had a larger proportion of shore duty than he; and that he had been kept at the Naval Observatory by the various Secretaries of the Navy because of his special fitness for the work. This latter statement was proved by personal letters, of which the following from William A. Graham will serve as an example: "In answer to your inquiry, why you were not ordered to sea during my connection with the Navy Department, I have to state that I considered your services at the National Observatory of far more importance and value to the country and the navy than any that could be rendered by an officer of your grade at sea in time of peace. Indeed, I doubt whether the triumphs of navigation and of the knowledge of the sea achieved under your superintendence of the Observatory will not contribute as much to an effective Naval Service and to the national fame as the brilliant trophies of our arms".

Resolutions in favor of Maury's restoration to the active service list were passed by the state legislatures of Tennessee, Louisiana, Alabama, Maryland, New Jersey, Virginia, and New York. Of those passed by the last-mentioned state, he wrote, "These resolutions uttered by a great state in the manner of a free people have a charm that is lacking in these honors which, in the shape of medals, orders of knighthood, crosses, and decorations, have been conferred by the hands of strangers".

Finally, in view of the findings of the court of inquiry and the sympathy for Maury which had been aroused throughout the whole country, the President not only restored him to the active service list but also promoted him to the rank of commander. The announcement of this promotion was as follows: "Sir: The President of the United States, by and with the advice and consent of the Senate, has appointed you a Commander in the Navy from the 14th of September, 1855, on the Active List. I have the pleasure to enclose herewith your commission, dated the 27th instant (January, 1858), the receipt of which you will acknowledge to the Department. I am respectfully, I. Toucey". Thus was Maury at last completely vindicated.

CHAPTER IX

Shadows of Coming Troubles

Though Maury emerged with victory perched upon his banners from his bitter conflict with the "Retiring Board", yet he was not to enjoy again the peaceful pursuit of scientific and philosophical researches. His mind was to be distracted by the consideration of a question which was before long to rend the country in twain and incidentally cause the wreck of his scientific ambitions.

Maury had always been distinctively a sympathizer in all the hopes and ambitions of the South, but he had early recognized the dangerous political potentialities in the slavery problem. As far back as 1850 he had set forth the free navigation of the Amazon River as a novel remedy for the preservation of the Union. According to his plan, Brazil was to become a country for the disposal of the surplus slaves of the South, and he hoped that in time by act of law slavery and involuntary servitude might be completely removed from the South. "The Southern states", he wrote, "may *emancipate* just as New York, Massachusetts, etc. emancipated their slaves—large numbers of them were not set free; they, after the acts of prospective emancipation became laws, were sold at the South; and so the South may sell to the Amazon and so get clear of them. In no other way can I see a chance for it,—the slaves of the South are worth about fifteen hundred million. Their value is increasing at the rate of thirty or forty million a year. It is the industrial capital of the South. Did ever a people con-

STATUE OF MAURY OVER THE MAIN ENTRANCE OF THE DEUTSCHE SEEWARTE (METEOROLOGICAL STATION OF THE GERMAN ADMIRALTY) IN HAMBURG

sent to sink so much industrial capital by emancipation or any other voluntary act?"

With characteristic energy Maury pressed the question upon the notice of the public. Lieutenant Lewis Herndon's report of his exploration of the Amazon Valley was submitted to Congress on January 26, 1853, and soon afterwards there appeared in the *National Intelligencer* and the *Union* of Washington at irregular intervals seven articles signed "Inca", in which the commercial, mineral, and agricultural potentialities of the Amazon region were painted in glowing colors. The free navigation of the Amazon River was demanded of Brazil by Maury in these "Inca" articles; and at the meeting of the Memphis Convention in June of the same year resolutions were adopted urging the same proposition. These resolutions were then reported to the House of Representatives in the form of a "Memorial of Lieutenant Maury in behalf of the Memphis Convention in favor of the free navigation of the Amazon River".

This propaganda made at first a very unfavorable impression on the Brazilians, and caused them to suspect that a scheme of annexation by the United States was the real reason for the insistence on the opening of their great river to free navigation. One Brazilian newspaper asserted that "this nation of pirates, like those of their race, wish to displace all the people of America who are not Anglo-Saxon". So strong was the feeling thus aroused that the House Committee on Foreign Affairs reported on February 23, 1855 that further action on the Maury memorial was for the present inexpedient. However, at last, on December 7, 1866, an agreement was signed providing that after September 7 of the following year the Amazon should be free to the merchant ships of all nations, as far as the frontier of Brazil.

Later even the Brazilians themselves conceded the beneficial influence of Maury in bringing this about. "After the publication in the *Correio Mercantil* of his (Maury's) memorial", wrote the Brazilian historian, Joaquim Nabuco,[1] "and his description of the Amazon region, locked up from the world by a policy more exclusive than Japan's or Dr. Francia's, the cause of the freedom of navigation was triumphant. Tavares Bastos himself received from the book by Maury the patriotic impulse which converted him into a champion of this great cause". Events moved too swiftly, however, in the United States for the development of the Amazon Valley to play any part in the settling of the slavery question.

Although Maury was, to a certain degree, pro-slavery and a strong States' rights man, yet he was by no means dis-unionist. In fact, during those critical months just preceding the outbreak of the War between the States he used all the power and influence at his command to keep the country united. As early as 1845 he referred in one of his letters to the "tendencies toward disunion in the nation", and as the years went by there was a constantly increasing number of references in his correspondence to the drifting of the ship of state toward the breakers. In his opinions regarding the great question at issue, he occupied a position in the middle ground and refused to permit himself to be carried away by either the extremists at the North or those of the South. He condemned with equal vigor the effort to

[1] *Um Estadista do Imperio* (Paris, 1897), III, 12.

precipitate the acquisition of Cuba, and John Brown's raid at Harper's Ferry. He believed that the people as a whole, both of the North and of the South, were not in sympathy with such schemes, but that such raids and filibustering expeditions were fostered by the unwisely partisan press, pulpit, and politicians.

He, therefore, suggested the calling of a council of *men out of politics*, ex-governors and old judges, from different states of the South to formulate some kind of a proposition to lay before the people of the North. "It will never do", he wrote, "to suffer this Union to drift into dissolution". With this end in view, he wrote to the governors of the border states, Pennsylvania, New Jersey, Maryland, and Delaware, to act as mediators.

His letter to Governor Packer of Pennsylvania will give an idea of what he hoped to accomplish. "When the affairs of a nation are disturbed", he declared, "quiet people, however humble their station, may be justified in stepping a little out of their usual way. In all exertions of duty, something is to be hazarded; and I am sure you have only time to hear what I wish to write—none to listen to apologies for venturing to write you this letter. You recollect that, in the nullification times of South Carolina, Virginia stepped forward as mediator, and sent her commissioners to that state with the happiest results. But we are now in the midst of a crisis, more alarming to the peace and integrity of the Union than those memorable times. We have the people, in no less than seven of those states, assembling or preparing to assemble in their sovereign capacity to decide in the most solemn manner known to them whether they will remain in the Union or no. The most remarkable feature in the whole case is, it appears to me, this—that here we have a national family of states that have lived together in unity for nearly three score years and ten, and that a portion of them are preparing to dissolve these family ties and break up the Union, because—because of what, sir? Ask legislators, ask governors, ask whom you will, and there are as many opinions as to the causes of discontent and the measures of redress as there are leaves in the forest. At no time have the people of any of the discontented states, acting in their sovereign capacity, ever authorized a remonstrance to be made to their sister states of the North against their course of action. We have heard a great deal of this from politicians, partisans, and others, but if the people of any one of the Southern states, acting in their sovereign capacity, have ever remonstrated with the people of the Northern states as to the causes of dissatisfaction and complaint, and thus laid the matter formally before you of the North, I cannot call it to mind. Neither has any Northern state so much as inquired of the people of any Southern state, either as to the cause of their offense or as to the terms and conditions upon which they would be willing to remain in the Union.

"It does appear to me that in and out of Congress we are all at sea with the troubles that are upon us; that the people, and the people alone, are capable of extricating us. You, my dear sir, and your state—not Congress—have it in your power to bring the people into the 'fair way' of doing this. This brings me to the point of my letter—then why will not the great state of Pennsylvania step forth as mediator between the sections? Authorize your commissioner to pledge the faith of his state that their ultimatum shall not only be laid before the people of the Keystone State, assembled likewise in their sovereign capacity, but that she will recommend it to her sister states of the North, for like action on their part, and so let the people, and not the politicians, decide whether this Union is to be broken up".

No tangible results, however, came from this effort, and Maury began to despair of the two sections' being able to arrive at a peaceable solution of the difficult problem. He had a clear conception of the nature of this fundamental question dividing the sections. "The disease", he wrote, "the root of the thing, is not in cotton or slavery, nor in the election of Lincoln. But it is deep down in the human heart. The real question is a question of Empire. And I do not think our political doctors will be able to treat the case upon any other diagnosis than this. The country is divided into sections; it is immaterial by what influence".

Meanwhile, Maury went about his work at the Observatory as well as he could with his mind distracted by the unsettled state of the country. In September, 1860, he made a visit with Mrs. Maury and other members of his family to Niagara Falls, and to Newburgh, New York to see the family of his old friend Hasbrouck. During the following month he went to Tennessee to speak at the laying of the corner stone of the University of the South at Sewanee, as has already been related. On this visit, Maury went to Nashville, where he delivered two speeches. One was to the school children on the subject of the sea; the other was before the same audience that heard Robert L. Yancey and on the same subject, the state of the country. Yancey urged war and made extravagant claims for success; but Maury counseled moderation and warned the people that danger was ahead. In November, he was in England whence he had gone to arrange for the copyrighting of a new edition of his "Physical Geography of the Sea".

During that month momentous happenings occurred in the United States. On November 6, Lincoln was elected President, and the day following the legislature of South Carolina took steps which resulted in the calling of a secession convention. This convention unanimously passed, on December 20, an ordinance declaring the state of South Carolina no longer in the Union.

By that time Maury had returned to the United States, and he made a last effort to secure mediation through Commodore Stockton as the representative of the Governor of New Jersey; but early in the year 1861 he sorrowfully wrote that the New Jersey plan had missed fire. After the failure of this attempt he sought in vain to be made a member of the "Peace Congress", which was called by the Border States and met in Washington in the month of February. In this he offered to represent Tennessee, which he referred to as his Naomi.

South Carolina had been followed out of the Union by Mississippi, Florida, Alabama, Georgia, Louisiana, and Texas. In February, the seceding states set up a provisional government with Montgomery as the capital and with Jefferson Davis as President and Alexander H. Stephens as Vice President. But Maury urged the "barrier" states, Virginia, Tennessee, and Kentucky, to remain in the Union in order to conserve the peace, to mediate, and to organize a re-annexation party for the next Presidential election.

On the day of Lincoln's inauguration, Maury wrote, "The new President is now on his way to the Capitol, and the *Express* reports 'All quiet', as I took it for granted it would be. I have no idea of any disturbance, or any attempt even at a plot. Of course, you will see the Inaugural as soon, if not sooner than I shall, for, having the telegraph, Mr. Lincoln may literally speak his polyglot through tongues of fire. Officers of the Army and Navy—should war come between the sections—will have a hard time; and, indeed, who will not? No military man can permit himself to accept service with a mental reservation. All who are foes of his flag, and whom his country considers enemies of hers, are enemies of his; therefore, if we have a war between the sections, every man who continues in 'Uncle Sam's' service, is, in good faith, bound to fight his own, if his own be on the other side. The line of duty, therefore, is to me clear—each one to follow his own state, if his own state goes to war; if not, he may remain to help on the work of reunion. If there be no war between the sections, we must hoist the flag of re-annexation, to carry the elections of '64 upon that issue, bring back the seceding states, and be happier and greater and more glorious than ever. As soon as the smoke clears away, you will see that the old party lines have been rubbed out. . . . Virginia is not at all ready to go out of this Union; and she is not going out for anything that is likely to occur short of coercion—such is my opinion".

But the broken fragments of the Union were not to be reunited in any such peaceful fashion, and Maury was soon to be forced to follow his native state into the bloody conflict. The overt act precipitating the war was the firing on Fort Sumter, April 12, 1861. Maury thought that the *Star of the West* with recruits for the garrison of the fort should not have been sent, for it was but an invitation to South Carolina to an overt act which would still further widen the breach between the sections.

In any case, the overt act came, when under fear of reinforcements from a strong squadron which was in preparation President Jefferson Davis on April 12, 1861 ordered General Beauregard to reduce Fort Sumter. Three days afterward President Lincoln issued a proclamation calling on the state governors to furnish 75,000 state militia. This caused Virginia to pass an ordinance of secession on the 17th of April. Moreover, in Tennessee, Maury's adopted state, sentiment favorable to the Confederacy began to crystallize, and on May 8 her legislature decided also in favor of separation from the Union and leagued the state with the Southern Confederacy. But in spite of the fact that Maury had written of Tennessee as his Naomi, it was his native Virginia that decided his future for him.

On the day this state passed her ordinance of secession, Maury wrote to his wife, who was visiting in Fredericksburg, not to return to Washington, for he expected Virginia soon to declare herself out of the Union and he would as a consequence immediately resign his commission in the navy. Three days later he regretfully forwarded to President Lincoln his resignation from the service in which he had spent so many happy and profitable years.

The circumstances connected with the writing of this resignation are thus related by Maury's daughter Mary: "It is related of Socrates that, when his last hour had come and one of his young disciples brought him the cup of hemlock, the young man covered his face with his mantle, weeping as he presented it, and, falling on his knees, he buried his face on the couch where his dear master sat awaiting his death. When Maury determined to leave the service of the United States, he bade his secretary (Mr. Thomas Harrison) write his resignation. That true and loyal heart, which had served and loved him for almost twenty years, and whose fluent pen had rendered him such willing service, refused its office now; and, presenting the unfinished paper with one hand, he covered his eyes with the other, and exclaimed, with a choking voice and gathering tears, 'I cannot write it, sir!' He knew it was the death-warrant to his scientific life—the cup of hemlock that would paralyze and kill him in his pursuit after the knowledge of nature and of nature's laws".

As far as the disturbed political conditions permitted, Maury continued his work at the Observatory down to the very day of his resignation, his last publications being Nautical Monographs, numbers 2 and 3, on "The Barometer at Sea" and "The Southeast Trade Winds of the Atlantic" respectively. With the war clouds gathering round him he had written, "What a comfort the sea is! I have withdrawn my mind from the heart-sickening scenes that you gentlemen are meeting". But with his leaving the Observatory this comfort was taken from him, and instead of the quiet contemplative life of a scientist he was to suffer for eight years the rough exigencies and trying uncertainties of the Civil War and its aftermath.

CHAPTER X

As His Friends and Family Knew Him Before the War

Before passing on to a consideration of Maury's connection with the events of the Civil War, one should give some attention to him as he appeared to his friends and family during the *ante bellum* decade when success, fame, and happiness were all his. Some idea of his personality has, perhaps, already been conveyed through the discussion of his work and achievements up to this point in his career, though only incidentally; now the aim will be to focus attention for awhile on Maury the man.

The range of his acquaintances was very extensive, and the list of his correspondents was largely the roll of the great men of his day. Among these were the following, taken at random: John Quincy Adams, John C. Calhoun, John Tyler, Leverrier and other astronomers both at home and abroad, Humboldt, the Grand Duke Constantine of Russia, the Archduke Ferdinand Maximilian of Austria, Jomard, the French Egyptologist, S. F. B. Morse, Cyrus W. Field, Professor Agassiz, Dr. Kane, Lord Wrottesley, Lord Ashburton, Bishop Otey, Bishop Leonidas Polk, Matthew Calbraith Perry, Nathaniel Hawthorne, Captain Jansen of Holland, Baron Justus von Liebig, John A. Dahlgren, William Gilmore Sims, Nathaniel Parker Willis, Michael Faraday, Benjamin Silliman, Jefferson Davis, Sam Houston, Donald McKay, and dozens of others whose names are not now so well remembered,—scientists, statesmen, and men of affairs. Maury's personality was

Courtesy of "The Journal of American History," Vol. IV, Number 3 (1910).

BUST OF MATTHEW FONTAINE MAURY BY E. V. VALENTINE, IN THE STATE
LIBRARY AT RICHMOND, VA.

such as easily to turn an acquaintance into a friend, and most of his friends, whether they were illustrious men or not, showed themselves to be friends indeed for they remained his friends in time of need, as will be seen in the later events of his life.

Now, as to the kind of man they found him to be, he was in the first place one who was remarkable for his great breadth of mind. The editor of the *Southern Literary Messenger* was of the opinion that Maury's astronomical researches had served to "enlarge all his perceptions and give greater breadth to all his views". That may be true, but he seemed to have had the natural capacity for taking a broad and extensive view of questions, some of which were world-wide in their scope. This is particularly noteworthy in his scientific researches, and his manifold extra-professional interests also amply exemplify the great sweep of his imaginative mind.

There was a certain charm to Maury's conversation and presence that drew people irresistibly to him. Nathaniel Parker Willis felt this charm. "He made me subject", wrote Willis, "to his personal magnetism, and while with him I had secretly vowed myself and my pen to the service of his interests and reputation thenceforward. . . . He was, unconsciously to himself, to me an exquisitely interesting study of character. I had long heard of him, and knew what the public generally knew of his pursuits; but my conviction was strengthened every day that he was greatly undervalued by common repute, and that he was of a far deeper intellect and much more of a natural philosopher than the world with all his repute gave him credit for. . . . Under his exceeding modesty and reserve, there seemed to be a vein of the *heroic* and romantic so hidden that he was seemingly unconscious of it, and I was quite sure before I parted with him that he was one of the *sans peur et sans reproche* class of men; yet willing to pass for only the industrious man of science which the world takes him for. Under the strong magnetism of his sincere and simple manner, I formed an irresistible attachment to him, and longed to set the world right as to his qualities".[1]

Some considered that the source of this charm lay in his strong and powerful imagination, which lifted him above the man of mere intellect and often lent the charm of eloquence to his conversation and to his lectures. Others were impressed with the simplicity and natural-ness of his character, which in its quiet unostentatious manner was very prepossessing. His manners were, indeed, as simple and unpretending as a child's, and he had as keen a relish for a joke as the jolliest Jack Tar that ever shipped with him.

Maury had a very modest estimate of his own work. He did not claim to have discovered anything. "I only bring together", he wrote, "the observations that others have made, and then leave it to the observations them-selves to discover their own meaning in their own way. Sometimes, indeed, I do become the mouthpiece of these observations and proclaim to the world what they reveal to me. But in this I consider myself merely as an in-strument. I am fortunate, indeed, when I succeed in rightly interpreting the meaning of the observations, and am happy always to find concurrence in the opinions expressed or entertained by older and wiser". His investigations on every subject were directed toward some practical benefit to his fellowmen, and he often

[1] In the *Home Journal* of New York, September, 1859.

quoted with appreciation the saying that he who made two blades of grass grow where only one had grown before was a benefactor to the world.

This practical attitude toward his work and toward life in general led Maury to have very definite ideas about education. These appeared to some extent in his scheme for a Naval School, but they were more fully revealed in his letters. Latin and Greek, he thought, should not be given the place of first importance as compared with mathematics and chemistry, and he declared that West Point was the only tolerable institution in the United States because of the absence there of the humbuggery of the Learned Languages. Female seminaries he considered to be "downright cheats" because of the superficiality of the knowledge imparted there. He was opposed to the neglect of the study of English, so prevalent in the schools and colleges of his day, and thought that Spanish, French, and German were languages well worthy of study. Naturally, he laid great stress on the value of mathematical, geographical, and other scientific studies. "As for the sciences", he declared, "more is now annually developed in every department thereof than was ever known, dreamed, or thought of, by the ancients".

Maury himself had been largely self-educated, but his speeches as well as his writings show that he had read widely and discriminatingly. He was well read not only in science and naval history and biography, but also in the classics, and often quoted passages from Shakespeare, Byron, Dante, and the Bible; in the course of a single speech he referred intelligently to Plato, Plutarch, Seneca, Goethe, Bacon, Newton, and other authors. He is said to have been fond of reading aloud to his family from Scott's novels and poems, Shakespeare's plays, and the works of many other British poets, particularly Wordsworth and Mrs. Hemans.

The Civil War interfered materially with the education of Maury's sons. His eldest son Richard spent some time at the University of Virginia, while John Herndon was placed in the Virginia Military Institute. This interference was a source of great disappointment to their father who had shown the keenest interest in their education, or, as he expressed it, "putting on their armor for the battle of life". This same cordial interest in young men is manifest in his addresses before college students, and appears frequently in his correspondence. One letter in particular is of great interest, in this connection, because of the light it throws on Maury's character as well as for its revelation of his ideas on education. The last portion of the letter, which was written to young Hamilton Lieber at the time he was on the point of entering the United States Naval Academy as a midshipman, is as follows: "Your future position in life and your standing in the navy depend upon the degree of energy with which you shall acquit yourself of the duties required of you as a Midshipman. If you be idle and inattentive now, you cannot hereafter recover the ground that you will lose. Letting the opportunities now afforded you pass unimproved, you cannot expect hereafter to contend, except at great odds, with your comrades for the honors of the profession.

"Make it a rule to make everything while you are young bend to your profession. The books that you read for amusement, let them be professional books instead of novels—which I hope you will *never* read— read the lives of eminent naval men. I commend to your particular attention Mackenzie's 'Life of Decatur' and the 'Life of Admiral Collingwood'.   Take these two characters as your examples, and always have them in your eye; make them in all things, except the duel and the course toward Barron, your models.

"I say never read novels, but eschew them while you are young as I hope you will strong drink—because they are as destructive to the wholesome habits of the mind as mint-juleps are to those of the body—they both enervate and unfit one for hard study or hard labor—and as a beverage both are very pleasant.   But hate them both, I pray you, my young friend, for they are poisons.

"Make it a rule to ask yourself at night what you have learned during the day, and do not be content until you get a reply, and always learn something if it be only the meaning of a word from the dictionary.

"Make it a rule to obey all orders promptly and cheerfully.   It is immaterial how disagreeable the officer giving the order may be, or how unpleasant the duty; go about it cheerfully, never sullenly nor carelessly. Sometimes you will find the Midshipmen disposed to turn on one of their fellows and 'run him' as it is called. Make it a rule never to join with them in this, for it not infrequently ends, particularly in the navy, in downright persecution.

"Make it a rule never to offend, nor to seek cause of offense in the conduct of others.   Be polite to all, familiar with but few.   Do not be quick to take offense; you will never find a gentleman who will willfully and without any cause, real or imaginary, offend another. Therefore whenever you imagine yourself aggrieved either by an equal or a superior officer—when you are in doubt as to whether the offense were intended or not, go straight up to him, state the case, and ask the meaning of the intention.   Never let imaginary offenses, slights, or cuts find a place in your breast—they sour the disposition.   Ask to have them explained at once, and in asking be always polite—never show temper,

"The rule in the navy is to treat everybody as a gentleman until he proves himself otherwise.   It is a good rule—observe it well.   You will sometimes hear the opinion expressed that it is necessary for a young officer to establish his courage by fighting.   Now believe me, my young friend, that the courage to stand up and be shot at is the poorest sort of courage.   He only is truly brave who has the courage to do right.   This is the highest quality of bravery that a military, or any other man can possess.

"The doing right, the acting up to the principle, may sometimes seem to you to be inexpedient, or it may have the appearance of making you unpopular—but this principle of conduct will build up a character founded on the rock which nothing can shake; and let me assure you that it is unwise and always wrong for a man to have enmity in his breast between himself and his conscience. When principle is involved, be deaf to expediency.   It is a dangerous word to all classes of men.   I would, if I could, teach you almost to hate it."

Now, a man who could attract and hold friends as Maury did would naturally be one whose family life was a happy one.   This, indeed, was true in his case. He was a faithful son who made his home that of his parents in their old age, a thoughtful and considerate brother to his sisters and brothers, even sharing his home for a time with his brother's widow and her children and often having other relatives under his roof. To his wife and children, Maury was their perfect ideal of a husband and father; while to him the happiest of all places was his home, and when he was away from it his mind was constantly filled with thoughts of his family. Many of his letters to friends contain references to his children, whose childish sayings he never tired of repeating.

His family, of course, knew Maury most intimately of all, and the following account of his appearance, personality, and home life is of particular interest and value: "Maury was a stout man, and about five feet six inches in height; he had a fresh, ruddy complexion, with curling brown hair, and clear, tender blue eyes. His massive head and strong neck surmounted broad and square shoulders, and a chest deep and full. His arms were long and strong, with hands small, soft, and beautifully formed—he was apt to use them in graceful gestures while conversing.

"Every feature and lineament of his bright countenance bespoke intellect, kindliness, and force of character. His fine blue eyes beamed from under his broad forehead with thought and emotion, while his flexible mouth smiled with the pleasure of imparting to others the ideas which were ever welling up in his active brain. In early manhood his head was well covered with fine soft, wavy brown hair, which became thin before he reached middle age. Latterly, he was quite bald, as is shown in Valentine's fine bust, taken when he was sixty years old.

"His conversation was enjoyed by all who ever met him; he listened and learned while he conversed, and adapted himself to every capacity. He especially delighted in the company of young people, to whom his

playful humor and gentle consideration made him very
winning.

"In his early youth he was careless in his dress, and
expressed contempt for those who judged of a man by his
outward appearance. 'But', he said, 'I soon perceived
the folly of this carelessness'; and in later years he became scrupulously neat in his attire. His enjoyment of
the pleasures of the table was refined; he liked good
wine; he carved well, and entertained generously; and
he was never more genial, humorous, or interesting than
when surrounded by friends about a well-served board".[2]

The account of his home life continues as follows:
"Whether writing or thinking, no noise of the children,
no invasion of visitors, was ever an interruption. In
the midst of his most interesting pursuits, on which he
was concentrating his powers, he would lay down his
pen and join in the laugh at a good joke, and encourage
the mirth to go on. He had an ever-active sense of
humor; but scandal and gossip he would not allow in
his presence, and he would never pass over any violation
of high principle. He made loving companions and
friends of his children—in his walks, in his talks, in his
work, in his recreation, he was always one of them. He
invited their confidence, and freely gave them his; in
that household there were no secrets—any step that was
about to be taken, any journey made, or any work projected, was fully and freely talked over and discussed in
family conclave. And yet his word was law; that no
one ever dreamt of disputing: so he was always the last
to speak in these family councils, and gave the 'casting
vote', as he used to say; the youngest voting or giving
their opinion first on the matter under discussion.

[2] *The Life of Maury* by Diana Fontaine Maury Corbin, pp. 147, 148.

"Most of his voluminous writings were thus freely submitted to the family council, or copied by them, and each one invited and encouraged to criticise; and thus, not only were they made familiar with the workings of his mind but were taught to express their own thoughts. He wrote or composed and dictated his greatest books in his parlor, surrounded by his family, and it seemed sometimes as if he possessed a dual consciousness, so quickly could he abstract or concentrate his mind upon his writing.

"Like few great men, he was the greater the closer one got to him.   Little children approached him confidingly, and never left him without bearing away some good lesson, so gently and simply taught as to be forever planted in their young minds.   His especial pleasure was to say a kind word and lend a helping hand to young men beginning the battle of life.   Above all men, he knew the value of praise as an incentive to high endeavor, and when he had occasion to censure or criticise, he did it with such obvious reluctance that it never failed to do the good intended.   While at home, he had been taught to respect women, to love the truth, and to reverence God; and these teachings he never forgot.

"One of his daughters writes as follows: 'He never had a study or anything like a sanctum, where his wife and children could not come, preferring to work in the midst of them wherever they congregated.   He would sit at the round marble-topped center table, with his papers spread out, the bright light falling on his bald head and shining on his brown curls, while he sat unconscious of what was going on around him; whether it was music, or dancing, or reading aloud, or romping, he would write away, or read what he had written, or talk to himself and shake his head'.

"His daughters often served as his amanuenses, and sometimes he dictated to two at once, while one of the little ones would balance herself on the rounds of his chair, and curl his back hair over the red-and-blue pencil he always used. Sometimes he would walk up and down the two parlors wrapped in a light blue silk Japanese dressing-gown, quilted with eider down, which was a present from Captain Jansen, the long ribbons, which should have been fastened around his waist, trailing behind him, or gathered up like reins in the hands of one of the little ones, who trotted after him, backwards and forwards, calling out 'Gee, woa!' or 'Back, sir!'— he paying not the slightest attention, but dictating gravely.

"He used to say he was the youngest of the family except the baby, and it was his habit, when dressing in the morning, to seat the youngest (the little two-year-old) upon the bureau, to hold the soap while he was shaving; while the rest would stand around, one to hold or receive the razor, one the brush, one the towel, and one or two the papers on which to wipe the razor; and we all would eagerly watch the pile of lather which he made with the soap and hot water in his shaving-can. He brushed his bald head with two immense brushes at the same time, one in each hand. 'For', he assured us gravely, 'you see, if I only use one at a time, it will turn me round and round like one oar in a boat'. And we believed that that was the only way to brush hair. Then he would tell us stories and anecdotes about his brothers and himself—what they did and what they said in Tennessee, and of his home life there. These stories he would tell over and over again, fitting them to the comprehension of the 'two-year-old', as she or he would come on, until we knew them by heart, and, with a clamor of tongues, would set him right if he omitted any incident or related it in the wrong order. And we knew exactly when to laugh and applaud, and enjoyed it all the more because it was so familiar.

"Often he would take the whole tribe out for long walks, or to gather fruit or nuts, or bright-colored leaves; and to reach the high ones he would make what he called a 'Tennessee arm', which was a long pole with a crutch at the end, with which he could twist them off, directing us where to stand and hold up our little pinafores to catch the coveted prize; and then what laughter and hurrahs and congratulations would be bestowed upon the fortunate catcher! He had pet names for all except the eldest; he said she grew up too fast for him to fit a name to her. There were 'Nannie Curly', 'Goggen', 'Davy Jones', 'Totts', 'Glum', 'Brave', and 'Sat Sing'. By these names he always called us, and we knew we had displeased him, and hung our heads with shame, if he gave us our baptismal ones.

"I don't think I ever went to school more than three months altogether. He was my loving and tender teacher always; and when Betty and I grew to be fifteen or thereabouts, we had to take care of one or two of the younger ones and teach them to read, write, and cipher, yet without allowing this duty to interfere with our own lessons or our regular tasks of sewing. He taught us our lessons at the breakfast table, and for an hour or so afterwards, his plan being to bid us—my sister Betty and myself—'one at a time, tell him about the lesson'. He seldom asked us questions on it, unless we found a difficulty in expressing ourselves, and he never asked those put down in the book. After both had had our say, he would, taking the lesson for a text, deliver the most delightful lectures. He prescribed no set time for our preparation of these lessons; but we were required to master them thoroughly, and give the substance to him clothed in our own words and not in those of the book. He always expected and required that we should not prepare them at night, but should then come into the parlor to receive and entertain and be entertained by the distinguished men and women who frequently gathered round him. He considered this a most important part of our education.

"He objected to the introduction of cards in the family circle, as he said they interfered with intelligent and improving conversation, and that those who had recourse to them for amusement were apt to depend on them, and could not exert themselves to be agreeable as they should and would do, if they had not this entertainment. He himself did not know one card from another. Our Mother taught us our Bible lessons and catechism, and she and Aunt Eliza, who was a beautiful needlewoman, gave us regular tasks in mending and darning. We seldom went to church more than once on Sunday, as it was so far from the Observatory to St. John's (Reverend Doctor Pynes); so Papa had us up regularly for the evening service, which we would read verse about, 'the stranger that was within our gates' generally taking part also. . . .

"He would never allow us to read works of fiction whilst we were students, and would punish most severely any departure from the truth, or act of disobedience. These two sins, he said, were the only ones he intended to punish his children for; and he was very careful not to make unnecessary issues with them, and never to give

an order unless he saw that it was obeyed and not forgotten. A punishment which he inflicted once on
Betty and myself I shall never forget. Betty borrowed
'Helen', one of a very handsome and complete set of
Miss Edgeworth's novels, from cousin Sally Fontaine
in Washington, thinking, or persuading herself, that
Papa would not object, as that was so mild a type of
fiction, and we both read most of it. He found us at
it one Saturday. He didn't say one word, but took
the book, and one of us in each hand, marched us down-
stairs into Mamma's room, and, to our horror, thrust
the handsome borrowed book into the flames, and held
it there with the tongs until it was entirely consumed.
Oh, how we did cry! It seemed such a terrible thing
to burn a book—a priceless book—of which we had so
few. Then our honor was touched to the quick, for we
had borrowed it. But for those very reasons the lesson
cut deep, and made the impression that was intended.
I for one would gladly have taken a whipping instead,
to be allowed to return the book uninjured".[3]

Whatever sternness Maury displayed toward his
children, it was so tempered with gentleness and loving
consideration that it did not detract at all from the ideal
relationship existing between them. When his two oldest daughters were married and left their father's home,
he saw to it that the loving ties which bound them to the
rest of the family were kept as strong as ever; and the
letters which he wrote to them were filled with the
tenderest and sincerest expressions of affection and the
most tactfully worded counsel and advice. For example,

[3] *Ibid.*, pp. 149–154. Maury's children were Betty, Diana Fontaine,
Richard Launcelot, John Herndon, Mary, Eliza, Matthew Fontaine, Jr.,
and Lucy.

he wrote to one of them, "That you are both poor is no ground of solicitude; happiness is above riches, and if you are not happy, being poor, wealth would not, I apprehend, make you happy. Poverty has its virtues, and my struggles with it are full of pleasant remembrances. I hope your experience will tally with mine. I do not say, strive to be content, for in that there is no progression; but be content to strive". At another time he wrote, "I am writing you a very disjointed letter, my love, but I have been thinking so much of you, and missing you so sorely, and loving you so tenderly, since you went away, and my heart was so full, and my head so empty, that I hardly know what I have said. Did you plant the yellow jasmine at Farleyvale? 'Tis the grand scion of the one I courted your Mother under, and I wish it, or a slip from it, to be planted over my grave". This request was carried out, and the flower grew over his grave for six or seven years until it was killed during an extremely cold winter. The entire story of Maury's home life seems almost too nearly perfect to be true, but diligent search of all available records has failed to disclose anything which would detract from the portrayal of him as always the true, considerate, loving husband and father.

Courtesy of Mrs. Thomas Fell and Mrs. C. Alphonso Smith.

MATTHEW FONTAINE MAURY AND THE REVEREND
DOCTOR TREMLETT

From a photograph made in Cambridge, England, in 1868, when Cambridge conferred the

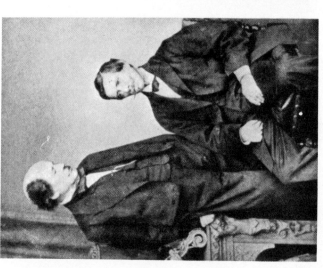

Courtesy of Mrs. Thomas Fell and Mrs. C. Alphonso Smith.

MATTHEW FONTAINE MAURY AND RAPHAEL
SEMMES

From a photograph made in London during
the War between the States.

CHAPTER XI

His Part in the Civil War: In Virginia

Maury resigned from the naval service and left the National Observatory on April 20, 1861. He declared that he worked as hard and as faithfully for Uncle Sam up to three o'clock of that day as he had ever done, and at that hour turned over all the public property and records of the office to Lieutenant Whiting, the officer who was next in authority. He left the Observatory with the deepest regret. "Its associations", he wrote, "the treasures there, which, with your help and that of thousands of other friendly hands, had been collected from the sea, were precious to me and as I turned my back upon the place a tear furrowed my cheek, for I could not but recollect that such things were".

From Richmond, on April 26th, he wrote to Secretary of the Navy, Gideon Welles, who had requested to know his reasons for his resignation, the following reply: "I am not aware of any law or rule that requires an officer tendering resignation to give reasons therefor. In this case, however, I have no objections to state them. They are these: our once glorious Union is gone; the state through which and for which I confessed allegiance to the Federal government has no longer any lot or part in it. Neither have I. I desire to go with my own people and with them to share the fortunes of our own state together. Such are the reasons for tendering my resignation, and I hope the President will consider them satisfactory". Maury afterwards stated in detail the reasons for his resignation in his "A Vindication of

143

Virginia and the South", which was the last thing that he prepared for the press, in May, 1871. This statement, which must be read as a whole in order to get the full force of his arguments, is much too long to quote here; but it is sufficient to say that his action was prompted by the same feelings and motives that inspired Lee and the dozens of other officers in both army and navy who went with their respective states when secession was decided upon. Furthermore, as will be seen later, in Maury's case the sacrifices involved were perhaps greater than those suffered by any other man who cast his lot with the South.

But, strangely, from the very beginning of the Civil War Maury's name was singled out for special condemnation, and many false statements were made about him and his work. He was accused of carrying on treasonable correspondence with the enemy before he resigned from the service, and of having the buoys removed from the Kettle Bottom Shoals and of taking away with him from the Observatory the maps of Georgia, Alabama, and Florida. His astronomical and meteorological work was ridiculously depreciated, and toward the close of the war the National Academy of Sciences went so far as to pass on January 9, 1864 this resolution: "Resolved by the National Academy of Sciences, That in the opinion of this Academy the volumes entitled 'Sailing Directions', heretofore issued to navigators from the Naval Observatory, and the wind and current charts which they are designed to illustrate and explain, embrace much which is unsound in philosophy and little that is practically useful, and that therefore these publications ought no longer to be issued in their present form". Among all the injuries which

Maury suffered from casting his fortunes with Virginia and the South, these hostile condemnations by former fellow officers and scientists, made in the midst of the animosities of civil strife, were perhaps the most damaging, for they cast a cloud upon his good name and the fame which he had won in the field of oceanography,—a cloud of misrepresentation which after more than half a century has not been entirely removed.

Upon Maury's arrival at Richmond, he lost no time in offering his services to Governor Letcher, who granted him a commission as commander in the Navy of Virginia, dated April 23, 1861. . At about the same time he appointed him a member of his Executive Council, only just authorized by an ordinance of April 20. Its other members were: Honorable John J. Allen, President of the Court of Appeals; Colonel Francis H. Smith, Superintendent of the Virginia Military Institute; R. L. Montague; and Thomas S. Haymond. This council, ordered to devise plans for the arming and protecting of the state in the shortest time possible, continued to function until June 19 of the same year, when its manuscript minutes come abruptly to a close. On April 25, Virginia had joined the Confederate States and adopted their provisional government; and on April 29 Richmond had become the Capital of the Confederacy. The Virginia State Navy was then incorporated with that of the Confederacy, and on June 10 Maury received his commission in the Confederate States Navy.

On the following day Maury wrote, "I begin to feel very useless. I am afraid there is too much red tape yet left in the world. I hope it may not tie us down". After remarking that there were small men in the Confederate government, and that there had been conflicts between Virginia authority and that of the Confederacy, he continued, "Davis, it appears to me, is grasping after patronage. Don't think he likes Lee. Lee told me yesterday he did not know where he was. Nor do I. I can see though how that may have proceeded from an honest misunderstanding. But it's bad in times like this to so jar your general that he does not know whether he is in or out of power. . . . Where the wrong is I am not so clear, but the biggest promotions seem to be on the other side. You may rely upon it, the Confederate States government has come here feeling that there is between it and us something of antagonism". Maury had reason to feel uncertain as to his standing, for Davis had been unfriendly to him when he was seeking vindication for the unjust action of the Retiring Board, and his strongest opponent at that time had been Mallory, then Chairman of the Senate Naval Affairs Committee and later Secretary of the Navy in the Confederate government. Besides, among the naval officers whom Maury had affronted during that unpleasant controversy was Buchanan, who had become the officer of highest rank in the Confederate Navy.

Maury had the affairs of his family on his mind also, and he was particularly concerned over his wife who had been made ill by the shock incident to the sudden outbreak of the war and the breaking up of her home in Washington. She and her younger children had, through the kindness of a cousin, John Minor, been taken into his home in Fredericksburg, a handsome brick house with a lovely garden, which still stands at 214 Main Street much as it appeared when the refugees occupied it. Here came also Maury's two married daughters with their children, Mrs. W. A. Maury with her one child from Washington, and Mrs. Corbin with her two children from her country place which was so near the Potomac that it soon fell into the hands of the Federals. His sons-in-law and his two eldest sons had early entered the Confederate army. His mind was greatly disturbed also because of his financial investments in the North, which had been made through his cousin Rutson Maury of New York and his friend Hasbrouck of Newburgh, New York. The latter remained a true friend in spite of the war, and at Maury's request was able to save a small part of his investments. Their relation, as effected by the war, is an example of the many that.existed of like nature, and its peculiar poignancy is indicated in this letter: "The nefarious Civil War that rages has not and I trust never may cool our hearts towards you and your dear family. My son Henry is an officer in the army of the North, he could not with honor decline to serve in it. Your son Richard is an officer in the army of the South, as you informed me in one of your letters, and could not probably with honor decline to serve in it. I sincerely hope that Henry and Richard may never meet in any battle during this unhappy war, and by duty and honor be obliged to shed each other's blood".

Maury, however, did not allow separation from his family and depression of spirts to interfere with the performance of what he considered his duty, but made an enthusiastic endeavor to make the most possible out of conditions as he found them. He first assisted in fortifying Jamestown Island in the James River and Gloucester Point on the York River, early in May, 1861, for the defense of Richmond. Besides he sat almost daily with the Governor's Executive Council to consider the many problems which confronted the State in her time of great need.   In the summer of 1861 he was appointed Chief of the "Naval Bureau of Coast, Harbor, and River Defense", and began to plan the construction of submarine mines to be placed in the rivers and harbors of the South. These were to be exploded under enemy ships by electricity, and insulated wire was needed for this purpose. He accordingly sent a Richmond merchant to New York to secure a large quantity of such wire.   The merchant failed in his mission, but Maury undismayed set about devising mines which could be exploded in a different way.   Each mine consisted of an oak cask filled with 200 pounds of powder, in the head of which was a trigger attached to a fuse.   The casks were joined together in pairs by 500 feet of rope, and when in a favorable position were let go to be carried by the tide down upon an enemy ship in such a way as to have the rope catch across the cable of the vessel.   As the mines drifted near the ship, the strain on the rope would release the triggers, ignite the fuses, and explode the mines.

Early in July, 1861, Maury himself commanded an expedition from Sewell's Point near Norfolk, which made an attempt to destroy the Union vessels *Minnesota*, *Roanoke*, and *Cumberland*, then off Fortress Monroe. The attacking party in five boats set off about ten o'clock.   Maury was in the first boat with the pilot and four oarsmen; while each of the others carried an officer and four men, together with one of the mines.   It was a very quiet Sunday evening, and as the enemy had no guard boats, the attacking party was able, under muffled oars, to take up a position near enough for their purpose just as seven bells struck on board the intended victims. The mines were immediately set adrift, and the boats

rowed away.   But no explosions followed, for something
had gone wrong with the mechanism of the mines.
Afterwards it was found that the type of fuse which had
been used would not burn in a pressure of twenty feet
of water, the depth at which the mines had been floated.
Later, the torpedoes, as they were then called, were
discovered by the Federals, taken out of the water, and
carried away as relics.

Maury was not overly discouraged, but returned to
Richmond to continue his experiments so as to perfect
an apparatus which would be more successful next time.
These experiments were made possible through the
assistance of the Richmond Medical College, which furnished batteries and offered the use of its laboratory,
and by the help of the Tredegar Iron Works as well as
those of Talbot and Son.   Maury carried on these experiments at the house of his cousin Robert H. Maury in
Richmond at 1105 East Clay Street, which was marked
in 1910 by the Confederate Memorial Society with this
commemorative inscription: "In this house, Matthew
Fontaine Maury, LL. D., U. S. N., C. S. N., invented
the submarine Electrical Torpedo, 1861–62".

While engaged in this work, Maury set forth his hopes
of success in the following letter: "I am experimenting
upon my deep sea batteries and so far, as difficulties have
presented themselves, they have one by one been overcome.   I shall be ready for demonstration next week I
hope. . . .   Then if I can get the powder, I will launch
in the Potomac, the Chesapeake, and its tributaries
hundreds of these things in pairs, each pair connected by
a line several hundred feet in length and in such a manner
that if the line fouls the vessel while she is at anchor, or
any vessel crosses the line while she is under weigh, the

tightening of the line will pull a trigger and let the things off. I think I can drive the enemy out of the Chesapeake. This is a business, this thing of blowing up men while they are asleep, that I don't glory in. . . . I shall endeavor to pick up and save the crews from drowning".

Maury was not given an opportunity to demonstrate his improved mine, until late in July or early in August, 1861, when the Secretary of the Navy, the Governor of Virginia, and the Chairman of the Committee of Naval Affairs consented to witness a trial on the James River at Rocketts, where the James River Steamboat Company's wharf is now located. Maury thus describes the trial: "I made a pair of submarine batteries. Your man Mallory pronounced them humbugs. I got him and Conrad (Chairman of Naval Affairs Committee, House of Representatives) to go and see them blow up the James River. I put them adrift aiming them at a buoy. They caught, drifted down, tightened the rope, pulled the trigger, and off they went blowing the river, or some of it, sky high and killing innumerable fish. So Mallory after that asked for an appropriation of $50,000 to enable me to go ahead".

This money was not, however, immediately forthcoming, and Maury complained that he was forced to lay on his oars and wait for the word from Congress, "Go ahead!" He also wrote that he was anxious to mine the river passes to both Richmond and Fredericksburg with these submarine batteries which would be exploded by electricity, but that lack of materials was delaying the project. During this delay, he planned another attack on the Union ships off Newport News. This materialized in an attempt which was made, on October 10, by

Lieutenant Robert D. Minor to sink the *Savannah* and the *Minnesota*, but this second trial also met with failure. Maury had planned to take part himself in the attack, but was prevented from doing so by his being ordered to Richmond with the expectation of being sent to mine the Mississippi River. He did not, however, go on this mission, though he had considerable correspondence with General Polk, who wished to place mines in the river at Columbus, Kentucky. Some mines were sent to Memphis with full instructions as to how they should be planted; and here others were constructed, after Maury's model, to be used elsewhere on the river.

About the first of May, 1862, Maury had the good fortune to secure ten miles of insulated wire which enabled him to mine the James River with electric mines, according to the plans which he had been compelled to lay aside for several months for lack of material. This wire had been used by the Federals in attempting to lay a submarine telegraph across the Chesapeake from Fortress Monroe to Eastville; but having been forced to abandon the attempt, they left the wire in the water and the waves cast it upon the beach near Norfolk where a friend, Dr. Morris, secured it for Maury's use.

The following report describes the mines that were then constructed and relates how they were laid down in the James River early in June, 1862: "The James River is mined with fifteen tanks below the iron battery at Chapin's (Chaffin's) Bluff. They are to be exploded by means of electricity. Four of the tanks contain 160 pounds of powder; the eleven others hold 70 pounds each. All are made of boiler plate. They are arranged in rows as per diagram, those of each row being 30 feet apart. Each tank is contained in a water-tight wooden cask, capable of floating it but anchored and held below the surface from three to eight feet, according to the state of the tide. The anchors of each are an 18-inch shell and a piece of kentledge, so placed as to prevent the barrels from fouling the buoy ropes at the change of the tide. Each shell of a row is connected with the one next to it by a stout rope thirty feet long and capable of lifting it in case the cask be carried away. The casks are water-tight, as are also the tanks, the electric cord entering through the same head.

"The wire for the return current from the battery is passed from shell to shell and along the connecting rope, which lies at the bottom. The wire that passes from cask to cask is stopped slack to the buoy rope from the shell up to the cask, to which it is securely seized to prevent any strain upon that part which enters the cask. The return wire is stopped in like manner down along the span to the next shell, as per the rough sketch. At 4 (in the sketch) the two cords are frapped together, loaded with trace chains a fathom apart, and carried ashore to the galvanic battery.

"For batteries we have 21 Wollastons, each trough containing eighteen pairs of plates, zinc and iron, ten by twelve inches. The first range is called 1, the second 2, and the third 3, and the wires are so labeled. Thus all of each range are exploded at once.

"Besides these, there are two ranges of two tanks each, planted opposite the battery at Chapin's Bluff. When they were planted, it was not known that a battery was to be erected below. These four tanks contain about 6,000 pounds of powder. The great freshet of last month carried away the wires that were to operate the first pair, 'A' (in a diagram enclosed, which showed the exact location of the various mines).

"Lieutenant Davidson, who with the *Teaser* and her crew has assisted me with a most hearty good will, has dragged for the tanks without success. They rest on the bottom. Could they be found, it was my intention to raise the four, examine them, and, if found in good order, place them below the range, 'I'.

"Lieutenant William L. Maury, assisted by Acting Master W. F. Carter and R. Rollins, was charged with the duty of proving the tanks and packing them in casks. There are eleven others, each containing 70 pounds of powder. When tested in the barrels and found ready for use, they will be held in reserve in case of accident to those already down. A larger number was not prepared, for the want of powder. There are a quantity of admirable insulated wire, a number of shells for anchors or torpedoes, and a sufficient quantity of chains for the wires remaining. They will be put in the navy store for safe-keeping. The galvanic batteries; viz., 21 Wollastons and 1 Cruikshank, the latter loaned by Dr. Maupin of the University of Virginia, with spare acids, sulphuric and nitric, are at Chapin's Bluff in charge of Acting Master Cheeney. He has also in jugs a sufficient quantity mixed to work the batteries, and ready to be poured in for use.

"It is proper that I should mention to the Department in terms of commendation the ready and valuable assistance afforded by Dr. Morris, president telegraph company, and his assistant, especially by Mr. Goldwell. My duties in connection with these batteries being thus closed, I have the honor to await your further orders".

Maury was relieved, on the 20th of June, 1862, by Lieutenant Hunter Davidson of the duty of "devising, placing, and superintending submarine batteries in the James River". Davidson was at the time in command of the *Teaser*, and to signalize his new appointment, he had the misfortune, on July 4, of losing his ship to the enemy, together with the diagrams showing the exact position of the mines already laid down.

Although Maury's participation in this new field of warfare had extended over only a little more than the first year of the war, still his pioneer work therein deserves high consideration as it laid the foundation for experiments by other Confederate officers, and these mines, electric and otherwise, resulted in the loss during the war of a large number of Union ships, varying from 20 to 58 according to different authorities. These facts bear out the following claim made by Maury: "All the electrical torpedoes in that (James) river were prepared and laid down either by myself or by Lieutenant Davidson who relieved me after having been instructed by me as to the details of the system. These were the first electrical torpedoes that were successfully used against an enemy in war".

Maury did not pretend that the idea was original with him. Robert Fulton had had a device for firing a mine by electricity, but had never succeeded in making his battery work. Also Colonel Colt experimented with some success with such mines as early as 1842. Maury's work was so important because he was the first to demonstrate that such weapons could be made of practical use in warfare. He has, however, been given almost no credit, until recently, for this pioneer work. Even Jefferson Davis, in his "Rise and Fall of the Confederate

Government", makes no mention of Maury's name in connection with the electric mines, but gives all the honor to General Gabriel J. Rains, who did not become head of the Torpedo Bureau until October, 1862. Scharf's "History of the Confederate States Navy" names not only Rains but also Hunter Davidson and Beverly Kennon as rivals for priority in the invention and practical use of the electric mine. The claims of the first two are so extravagant and so unjust to Maury as to merit no consideration; while those of Kennon cannot be successfully sustained in comparison with the well-established priority of Maury's "electrical torpedoes".

These electric mines were not the only new naval weapons that Maury advocated and had a hand in devising. In the autumn of 1861, he wrote a series of articles for the Richmond *Enquirer* under the pseudonym of "Ben Bow", in which he urged the necessity of building a strong navy for the South without delay, and of providing, at least, for the protection of bays and rivers by the construction of small ships armed with big guns. Maury had had in mind such a fighting craft for years, and as early as 1841 he had urged the building of ships of this sort in his "Scraps from the Lucky Bag".

In these "Ben Bow" articles he called attention to the fact that the Confederate government had not as yet realized the need for a navy. "The sums appropriated by the Government", he wrote, "for *building and increase* will indicate its policy touching a navy, and show what, for the present, is proposed to be done. Two Navy Bills have passed since Virginia seceded and joined the Confederacy. One was passed in May at Montgomery, and the other in Richmond in August. In the Montgomery Bill there is not one dime for construction or increase. The whole appropriation is $278,500, of which $100,000 is for equipment and repairs. Now a navy without vessels is like lamps without oil. The Richmond Bill gives $50,000 to buy and build steamers and gunboats for coast defense, and $160,000 for two ironclad gunboats for the defense of the Mississippi River and the city of Memphis. . . . We may safely infer that $50,000 will neither purchase nor build a great many steamers or gunboats, nor enable us to provide very efficiently for the defense of all the rivers except the Mississippi, and of all the harbors, bays, creeks, and sounds of our coast all the way from Washington on the Potomac to Brownsville on the Rio Grande. Thus we perceive that since Virginia and North Carolina, with their defenseless, open, and inviting sea-front, seceded, the sum of only $50,000 has been voted towards the 'purchase or construction' of a navy, for the defense of the entire seacoast of the Confederacy! From this analysis, and from all that we can see doing on the water, it appears that the Government has not yet decided to have a navy".

It was a mistake, he thought, to believe that there was a magic power in cotton, that "Cotton is King" and could do all and more than it was possible for a navy to accomplish. Along this line, he declared, "There seems to be a vague idea floating in the public mind of the South that, somehow or other, cotton is to enable us to do, if not entirely, at least to a great degree, what other nations require armies and navies to accomplish for them. Because cotton-wool is essential to the industry of certain people, and because we are the chief growers of cotton-wool, therefore, say these political dreamers, we can so treat cotton, in a diplomatic way, as both to enforce

obedience to our revenue laws at home and secure respect to our citizens abroad.   But can we?   Did ever
unprotected wealth secure immunity to its owner?   In
the first place, cotton becomes, when handled in any
other way than the regular commercial way, a two-
edged sword, as apt to wound producer as consumer.
Every obstacle, which we place between it and the channels of commerce here, operates as a bounty for its pro-
duction elsewhere.   It is a very current but mistaken
idea to suppose that this is the only country in the
world properly adapted to the cultivation of cotton.   No
such thing.   Should even the present paper blockade
continue for a few years, and cotton rule at the present
New York prices of 22 cents, or even at 15 cents, our
political dreamers may wake up and find the cotton
scepter, if not entirely lost to our hold, at least divided
in our hand. . . . Suppose England and France do not
choose for a few months to come to break this paper
blockade, which we have not the naval strength to force,
paper though it be, does it follow that that blockade,
weak and ineffectual as, up to this time, it has notoriously been, will continue so until those nations get ready
to act?   The amount appropriated for the Lincoln navy
during the current year is upwards of $40,000,000. . . .
We cannot, either with cotton or with all the agricultural
staples of the Confederacy put together, adopt any
course which will make cotton and trade stand us as a
nation in the stead of a navy".

Then followed his statement as to the kind of war
vessels that were needed to give the Confederacy command, at least, of its own waters, and at an expense of
no more than three million dollars.   "In this change of
circumstances", he wrote, "it so happens that the navy

which we most require is for smooth water and shallow places. Such a one, consisting of small vessels, can be quickly and cheaply built. We want at once a navy for our rivers and creeks and bays and sounds; a navy consisting chiefly of vessels that, for the most part, will only be required to keep the sea for a few days at a time." These ships would be so small as to present little more than a feather-edge as a target to the enemy, and therefore be more invulnerable than the best shot-proof men-of-war. They would be not more than twenty or twenty-five feet broad, and with coal, crew, and guns aboard would float only two or three feet above the surface of the water. They were, in fact, to be really nothing but floating gun carriages, propelled by steam, and each was to carry two rifled cannon of the largest caliber. Such a ship would be able to engage, at long range, one of the largest ships of the Union navy, the *Minnesota*, for example; and in attacking head on, she would present a target of but forty square feet as compared with one of six thousand square feet of the *Minnesota*. This, at a distance of two or three miles, would be a great advantage to the smaller vessel. Maury claimed for this type of ship facility of construction, rapidity in equipment, economy in outfit, and efficiency in battle. The cost of one hundred of these small vessels, including armament, engine, and machinery, he estimated, would be $10,000 each.

This dogma of "big guns and little ships" made a very favorable impression on Governor Letcher and other prominent Virginians, and so Maury decided to bring the matter of their construction before the state government. But beyond his expectation, his plan met with favor in the Confederate Congress, which took over from the state of Virginia the support of the measure by passing two acts on December 23, 1861. These authorized the construction of not more than a hundred of the gunboats, according to a plan submitted by Maury and approved by a board of naval officers, and provided also $2,000,000 for that purpose.

Maury set to work superintending the building of the gunboats on the Rappahannock and at Norfolk. They were 21 feet in beam and 112 feet in length, and drew six feet of water. Their armament consisted of a 9-inch gun forward and a 32-pounder aft, and each carried a crew of forty men. By the middle of April, 1862, Maury expected to have the last hull ready for the machinery and guns. But delay was occasioned through the difficulty of procuring materials, both iron and wood, and steam engines, and also by the lack of a sufficient number of mechanics. Meanwhile the *Merrimac*[1] (C. S. S. *Virginia*) had demonstrated the great possibilities of iron-plated rams, and the Confederate Congress authorized, on March 17, 1862, the discontinuance of all such construction of wooden gunboats as might retard the building of ironclad rams.

Secretary of the Navy Mallory, who had not warmly

[1] Maury had some connection with the reconstruction of this vessel. In a lecture on "Man's Power-giving Knowledge", delivered by him to Virginia Military Institute students on January 23, 1871, he said, "After the burning of the Norfolk Navy Yard in 1861, the Governor's Council advised that the *Merrimac* should be raised and converted into an ironclad. Quick to perceive and prompt to act, as in the emergencies of the war he ever was, his Excellency caused it to be done". This is corroborated by the following entry in the minutes of the Council for May 11, 1861, for a meeting at which Maury was present: "Governor submitted for approval a proposal of B. and I. Baker of Norfolk to raise the wreck of the steamer *Merrimac* and deliver her in the Dry Dock at Gosport Navy Yard for $5000. . . . Advised unanimously that the proposed be accepted".

supported Maury's scheme, then suggested to President Davis that the fifteen already commenced be finished according to the original design, but that the remainder of the appropriation be diverted to the building of iron-clads. A few days later Maury wrote, "All my gunboats are to be converted into shot proof or abandoned". Thus ended in comparative failure this ambitious experiment, one that was very dear to Maury. That he held Mallory very much to blame is evident from the following: "The administration is gravely proposing to build here at Richmond a navy to go down and capture Fortress Monroe! Mal. proposed the other day that I should undertake to build such a navy, asserting that it could be done. That, I should say, is a considerable stirring up. Less than a year ago, I was to be banished for advocating a navy. Now since all our naval waters have been taken away and we have nowhere to float a navy, yet we are to have a navy to take the strongest fortress in America. Hurra for Mal.!"

There were many others besides Maury who considered that Mallory's administration of the Navy Department was inefficient. This is clearly shown by the fact that, on August 27, 1862, the Confederate Congress ordered a joint special committee of both houses to investigate the affairs of this department of the government. Its investigations extended from September 4, 1862 until March 24, 1863, and developed a great deal of evidence of inefficient management; but Mallory was too strong politically to be ousted from his position. Another severe critic of the Secretary of the Navy is Pollard who, in remarking on the great energy which the North from the beginning of the war displayed in naval preparations, declared, "The Confederate government showed a singular apathy with respect to any work of defense. The Confederate Congress had made large appropriations for the construction of gunboats on the Mississippi waters; there was the best navy-yard on the continent opposite Norfolk; there were valuable armories with their machinery at Richmond; and although the Confederate government was very far from competing with the naval resources of the enemy, yet there is no doubt, with the means and appliances at hand, it might have created a considerable fleet. In no respect was the improvidence of the government more forcibly illustrated than in the administration of its naval affairs; or its unfortunate choice of ministers more signally displayed than in the selection for Secretary of the Navy of Mr. Mallory of Florida, a notoriously weak man who was slow and blundering in his office and a butt in Congress for his ignorance of the river geography of the country".[2]

Soon after the moving of the Confederate capital to Richmond, Maury began to feel himself out of sympathy with the Southern political leaders. A week or so after the battle of Manassas he wrote that he had wished an offer of peace to be made after that victory, but that the politicians who had become generals wanted to increase their military reputation and had opposed such a step. He went so far as to draw up a peace message which he showed to the Governor of Virginia and other influential men. But it bore no fruit. "My peace message", he declared, "is to go, I understand, after the next great victory. May it come soon!" He did not have a very high opinion of Davis's statesmanship in those early months of the war, but considered him haughty and self-

[2] "The Lost Cause" by Edward A. Pollard, p. 192.

willed, and surrounded by shallow men whom he was using to further his own future re-election. He was particularly incensed with the inability of the administration to appreciate the importance of a navy, and he feared that, by ignoring this service, they would permit Virginia to be degraded. There was talk, he declared, of making New Orleans or Charleston the money capital, and that the government was run on the theory that the Confederacy belonged to Cottondom and that Cotton meant to rule.

Maury's strongest censures of Mallory and Davis were made during the November following the publication of his "Ben Bow" articles, which became so distasteful to Mallory and so alarming to his political ease of mind that he began to wish that Maury was entirely out of the country. Only a few days after the appearance of the first of these articles, he informed its author that he was to go to Cuba to purchase arms and other war materials, and said to him that in his judgment he could be better spared than any other officer in either army or navy. This intention was not, however, carried into effect; but Mallory continued to trifle with Maury and to prevent him from rendering any worthy service to the South.

At about this time, Maury received from the Grand Duke Constantine an invitation to come to Russia and make his home there under the patronage of that government. The letter, which was brought to Richmond under a flag of truce by the Russian minister, was as follows: "The news of your having left a service which is so much indebted to your great and successful labors has made a very painful impression on me and my companions-in-arms. Your indefatigable researches have unveiled the great laws which rule the winds and currents of the ocean, and have placed your name amongst those which will ever be mentioned with feelings of gratitude and respect, not only by professional men, but by all those who pride themselves in the great and noble attainments of the human race.   That your name is well-known in Russia I need scarcely add, and though 'barbarians', as we are still sometimes called, we have been taught to honor in your person disinterested and eminent services to science and mankind.   Sincerely deploring the inactivity into which the present political whirlpool in your country has plunged you, I deem myself called upon to invite you to take up your residence in this country, where you may in peace continue your favorite and useful occupations.

"Your position here will be a perfectly independent one; you will be bound by no conditions or engagements; and you will always be at liberty to steer home across the ocean in the event of your not preferring to cast anchor in our remote corner of the Baltic.

"As regards your material welfare, I beg to assure you that everything will be done by me to make your new home comfortable and agreeable; whilst at the same time, the necessary means will be offered you to enable you to continue your scientific pursuits in the way you have been accustomed to.   I shall now be awaiting your reply, hoping to have the pleasure of seeing here so distinguished an officer, whose personal acquaintance it has always been my desire to make, and whom Russia will be proud to welcome on her soil".

This invitation, coming at a time when Maury was being thwarted in his efforts to serve the Confederacy, must have been a great temptation.   But he did not hesitate in declining the offer; he had cast his lot with

Virginia and through her with the Confederacy. One of his daughters relates how he came to Fredericksburg to tell his wife and children of the offer and its rejection. There were two letters. "One was from His Imperial Highness, the Grand Duke Constantine, Grand Admiral of Russia", she wrote, "and one from Baron Stoeckle, Russian Ambassador in Washington, telling him how and by what route he was to travel to Russia, where he was to go for passports, money, advice, and information. My father was now fifty-seven years old. Every maritime nation of Europe had given him evidences of their appreciation of the benefits that their commerce had received from the use of his Wind and Current Charts and Sailing Directions. He read that correspondence to us in my mother's bedroom, all of us gathered around him, before the wood fire, the young ones leaning against him looking into his face with eager questioning eyes as he read that princely offer, and told us he would not go".

In his courteous reply to this generous invitation, Maury wrote that it was only his stern sense of duty that enabled him to withstand such inducements as none but the most magnanimous of princes could offer,—the hospitalities of a great and powerful Empire, with the Grand Admiral of its fleets for patron and friend. He assured the Grand Duke that he was grateful for the offer of a home on the banks of the Neva, where, in the midst of books and surrounded by his family and friends, he would be free from anxiety as to the future and have the most princely means and facilities for prosecuting those studies and continuing those philosophical labors in which he had taken so much delight in former years in Washington. He then reviewed the recent events that had taken place in the United States, and explained why he had followed the fortunes of Virginia. "The path of duty and of honor", he wrote in closing, "is therefore plain. By following it with the devotion and loyalty of a true sailor I shall, I am persuaded, have the glorious and proud recompense that is contained in the 'well done' of the Grand Admiral and his noble companions-in-arms. When the invader is expelled, and as soon thereafter as the State will grant me leave, I promise myself the pleasure of a trip across the Atlantic, and shall hasten to Russia that I may there in person, on the banks of the Neva, have the honor and the pleasure of expressing to her Grand Admiral the sentiments of respect and esteem with which his oft-repeated acts of kindness, and the generous encouragement that he has afforded me in the pursuits of science have inspired his—Obedient servant, M. F. Maury, Commander, C. S. Navy".

In this decision, Maury acted like another great scientist, Louis Pasteur who, when he was offered a professorship in Italy in 1871 during the Commune, would not leave France but said, "I should consider myself a criminal deserving a penalty for desertion if I left my country in her unhappiness to seek a better paid position than she can give me".

In March, 1862, Maury began to take a hand in the foreign affairs of the Confederacy. At this time he submitted to Colonel Orr, Chairman of the Senate Committee on Foreign Affairs, a paper setting forth the basis of a treaty with France. About a week later he wrote a long letter to Captain De Le Marche, Depot de la Marine, Paris, stating the commercial reasons why France ought to recognize the Confederacy; and these reasons were presented to President Davis for his consideration. In April, the French minister, accompanied by the Prussian envoy to the United States, came to Richmond under a flag of truce to pay in person his respects to Maury, and to deliver to him an invitation from Emperor Napoleon to come to France to reside.

In view of this correspondence as well as many other letters which he wrote to influential people in both France and Great Britain, and because of the evidence of the high esteem for him that was shown by the Grand Duke Constantine and the Emperor Napoleon, it was natural that he came to be considered a suitable representative of the South in some foreign country. As early as April, 1862 he was approached with the offer of a mission to Europe to fit out armed cruisers; but time dragged on without the matter being brought to a conclusion. He repeatedly requested of Mallory some active service, as he did not wish to be a drone; and was told by the Secretary that he thought he would be of use doing nothing. In August, Mallory did at last offer him the command of a gunboat at Charleston, but this Maury declined as the vessel could not go to sea and was intended merely for harbor defense.

Finally, in September, Maury was ordered to England on "special service". That he was not pleased with this duty under the conditions according to which he was supposed to work is revealed in the following letter, which he wrote after the close of the war: "I was sent here really to be got out of the way, but nominally to superintend contracts with men of straw who could not pay their hotel bills but who had made pretended contracts with the Navy Department for about fifty million dollars and who never did anything. There was a great desire to have me in the Navy Department and Mallory was afraid he'd be turned out. Therefore he sent me here with hands tied, and what I did I took the responsibility a la Tennessee."

With little enthusiasm, therefore, Maury made his preparations for departure to England. He was saddened by the necessity of parting from his family who had already begun to suffer from the fortunes of war. They had been driven from their refuge in Fredericksburg when that place was captured by Union troops on April 18, 1862, and on the following 1st of June his son Richard had his horse shot from under him in battle and was himself severely wounded. But obedient to the call of duty, he bade farewell to his family who were then making their home with relatives in Albemarle County and, with his youngest son, Matthew Fontaine, Jr., he set out for Charleston to take ship as soon as practicable for his new field of work.

CHAPTER XII

His Part in the Civil War: In England

Though Maury arrived in Charleston the latter part of September, it was not until October 12, 1862 that he departed with his twelve year old son "Brave" on board the steamer *Herald* to run the Union blockade. An attempt had been made some three days before and had been unsuccessful, as the vessel had run into an enemy sloop of war and was forced to put back within the protection of the forts. The second trial was successful, but it almost ended in disaster. "We crossed the bar once", Maury wrote, "and when we got in about two miles of the enemy the pilots plumped the ship ashore, where she lay all night. In the morning they opened on her but she got off without damage". Maury certainly could not have looked upon capture with any feelings of pleasure, but to reassure his wife he wrote, before leaving Charleston, "If we get caught, I expect soon to be exchanged. The Brave and I will have a bully time in prison".

Nothing further of an unusual nature happened on the six hundred miles voyage to the Bermudas except that Captain Louis M. Coxetter, who had never before been very far from land, after groping about for the island had to admit on the sixth day that he was lost.

James Morris Morgan, who as a midshipman accompanied Maury to England, thus relates how the great scientist extricated the captain from his difficulty: "He (Coxetter) told Commodore Maury that something terrible must have happened, as he had sailed his ship

directly over the spot where the Bermuda Islands ought
to be! Commodore Maury told him that he could do
nothing for him before ten o'clock that night and advised
him to slow down. At ten o'clock the great scientist
and geographer went on deck and took observations, at
times lying flat on his back, sextant in hand, as he made
measurements of the stars. When he had finished his
calculations, he gave the captain a course and told him
that by steering it at a certain speed he would sight the
light at Port Hamilton by two o'clock in the morning.
No one turned into his bunk that night except the
Commodore and his little son; the rest of us were too
anxious. Four bells struck and no light was in sight.
Five minutes more passed and still not a sign of it; then
grumbling commenced, and the passengers generally
agreed with the man who expressed the opinion that
there was too much d....d science on board and that
we should all be on our way to Fort Lafayette in New
York Harbor as soon as day broke. At ten minutes
past two the masthead lookout sang out, 'Light ho!'—
and the learned old Commodore's reputation as a navigator was saved".[1]

Fortunately Commodore Wilkes's squadron, which
had been hovering about the islands and overhauling all
the ships that passed, had just departed and the
Herald made her way unmolested into the harbor. Here
Maury remained for more than two weeks, waiting for
the Royal Mail Steamer *Delta* from St. Thomas. During
this time he was received as a private citizen and world-
renowned scientist by the governor of the islands, and
was called upon by the commandant of Fort St. George

[1] "Recollections of a Rebel Reefer", p. 100.

and honored with a dinner on board H. M. S. *Immortality* then stationed at Port Hamilton.

When the English ship sailed, she was followed to sea by the U. S. Sloops of War *San Jacinto* and *Mohican* in a threatening manner as though about to repeat the "Trent Affair" and take Maury from the vessel; but nothing of the sort materialized. At Halifax, where Maury arrived November 9, he received the most distinguished consideration from the general commanding the troops, the admiral of the fleet, and the governor of Nova Scotia. The Confederate flag was flown from the top of the hotel in his honor, and the hand-organs ground "Dixie" under his window all day.

Here Maury's party took passage, on November 13, on the Cunard Steamer *Arabia*, a paddlewheel full-rigged ship plying between Liverpool and Boston. The ship tumbled about considerably during a great part of the voyage, and Maury was "as seasick and amiable as usual". The voyage was uneventful, and Liverpool was reached in safety.

On arrival, Maury conferred with Captain James T. Bulloch, C. S. Navy, who had an office with Fraser, Trenholm, and Company, the financial agents of the Confederate government, at No. 10 Rumford Place. After a short stay in Liverpool, he went on to London to a house in Sackville Street which had already been engaged for him, where, according to Morgan, "All day long there would be in front of the house a string of carriages with coronets on their doors, while their owners were paying their respects to the great 'Lieutenant Maury'". Early in 1863, Maury established himself at Bowdon, a village about nine miles from Manchester,

From James Morris Morgan's "Recollections of a Rebel Reefer."

C. S. CRUISER "GEORGIA"

so that he could be near his son whom he had placed there in the Rose Hill School.

At the time of Maury's arrival in England, there were, it appears, eight officers of the Confederate Navy in Europe, who were engaged in the task of securing by whatever means possible the much needed ships for the Confederacy. Captain Samuel Barron, who had been sent over to command the ironclad rams at that time being built by Lairds at Liverpool, was the flag-officer and in actual command, though the duties and responsibilities of the various officers were not very clearly defined and often overlapped.

Maury's first accomplishment was the purchase, in March, 1863, of a new iron screw-steamer of about 560 tons, which had just been completed at Dumbarton on the Clyde. She was fitted out as a merchant steamer under the name of the *Japan*, and on April 1, set sail, pretending to be bound for the East Indies. At about the same time a small steamer, the *Alar*, cleared from New Haven for St. Malo with Commander William Lewis Maury and a staff of officers together with guns, ammunition, and other supplies. The two ships met off Ushant, where the war material was placed on board the larger vessel. Commander Maury, a cousin to M. F. Maury, then commissioned her a Confederate man-of-war with the name *Georgia*.

The ship at once began a cruise which lasted seven months and resulted in the capture of eight or nine vessels, amounting to a loss of $406,000. After cruising over the South Atlantic and calling at Bahia, Brazil, where she fell in with the *Alabama*, and at Capetown, she made her way in safety to Cherbourg, France, where she arrived during the night of October 28–29. Here

Commander Maury was detached because of ill health, and the ship was refitted. But she was fated not to go out on another cruise. The vessel was not adapted to the service for which she was required; her coal capacity was limited and the consumption of fuel on her was made very large because she lacked great sail-power and always had to chase under steam. She did, however, slip out past the Union ships on guard, and made her way to the Mediterranean to a rendezvous with the C. S. S. *Rappahannock* on the coast of Morocco. Here her battery, ammunition, and a part of her crew were to be transferred to the other vessel, and she was then to be sold. But the French kept such a close watch on the *Rappahannock* that she was not able to leave the harbor of Calais, and the *Georgia* was at last forced to turn about and make her way to Bordeaux. She was then ordered to Liverpool, where on the 10th of May, 1864, she was put out of commission and sold to an Englishman by the name of Edward Bates for about 15,000 pounds. She was then captured in August of that year by Captain T. T. Craven of the U. S. S. *Niagara*, and sent to Boston, where she was condemned; and afterwards the owner's claim for damages was disallowed by the Mixed Commission at Washington.

Maury was instructed by the Secretary of the Navy, on June 8, 1863, to purchase another ship. This order, however, did not reach him until two months afterwards, and he was not able to carry it out until the month of November, when he secured a condemned dispatch boat belonging to the Royal Navy. This was the *Victor*, a screw-steamer of about 500 tons which had been offered for sale at Sherness. For fear of being stopped, Maury hurried her to sea on the wintry night of November 24,

with workmen still on board and with only a few of her
intended crew.   Her officers joined her in the Channel,
where she was commissioned the *Rappahannock*.   Two
days later she entered the harbor of Calais under the
guise of a Confederate ship in distress.   Here the
French threw such restrictions about her as to prevent
her from even making an attempt to leave port.   Some
endeavors were made to sell the vessel, but the war came
to an end before this could be accomplished and the ship
was eventually turned over to the United States.   Her
commanding officer had considered her a poor ship for
commerce destroying, because her machinery took up
too much space and her magazine was so large as to leave
but little room for crew and provisions.   The ship was
often referred to as "The Confederate White Elephant",
but she did serve the very useful purpose of keeping
two United States war vessels constantly off Calais to
prevent her from going to sea.

Maury and the other Confederate agents had great
obstacles to meet in securing ships, and probably did as
well as possible under the circumstances.   Federal
agents were constantly on the watch to see that French
and British neutrality was strictly observed, and besides
Maury and his associates were greatly handicapped by
the lack of money for the purchase of vessels and the
insufficiency of both officers and their crews.   "If I had
had money and officers", wrote Maury, "I could since I
have been here have fitted out half a dozen just as good
to prey upon the Yankee commerce as the *Alabama*".

Maury also had a hand in the attempt to have two
ironclad rams constructed in a French port for the Confederate government, one of which he hoped to have the
privilege of commanding.   The specifications for such

vessels were these: ability to cross the Atlantic, hulls of wood and iron with two armored turrets, engines of 300 horsepower which would give great momentum and a speed of fifteen or sixteen knots, two twin screw propellers, and a draft of fifteen feet.   His general plan and the cost of construction were approved by Secretary Mallory, and on July 16, 1863 the contract was signed between Bulloch and L. Arman, a naval constructor at Bordeaux, for the building of the two steam rams.   But these ships of war were destined never to be finished for the Confederacy, for the turn of events in America and the attitude of Great Britain caused the Emperor Napoleon to shift his position diplomatically and maintain a strict neutrality, though at one time, according to Maury's diary, the Emperor had written to Arman for a description of the guns with which the rams were to be armed in order that the French government might superintend their fabrication, and test them to see if they were properly constructed.

Maury was engaged in other activities in England and on the Continent which were altogether political in their nature.   He had a European reputation for his literary and scientific attainments, and was peculiarly well qualified to bring the Southern version of the causes, progress, and probable outcome of the war before an influential class of people.   Upon his arrival in England he began at once to exert this influence, both privately and publicly.   As an example of the latter form of propaganda was a letter which he addressed to the editor of the London *Times*.   This appeared in that newspaper on December 22, 1862, and set forth a sanguine account of conditions in the South as he had recently seen them, and sought to impress upon the British the hopefulness of the Southern cause.

On October 7 of that year, Gladstone, the Chancellor of the Exchequer, had said at a banquet at Newcastle, "There is no doubt that Jefferson Davis and other leaders of the South have made an army; they are making, it appears, a navy; and they have made, what is more than either—they have made a nation". The speech caused a sensation, and was received with cheers. "We may anticipate", he also declared, "with certainty the success of the Southern States so far as their separation from the North is concerned".[2] Maury had reason, therefore, for being at first very hopeful of European recognition and intervention, and was not merely drawing on his imagination when he wrote, "The Emperor may, and I hope will, decide on recognition and there are hopes here that when Parliament meets, February 5, the British government may find itself compelled to do something".

In a short time, however, his eyes began to be opened, and he saw that, though great admiration was expressed for the bravery of the soldiers and the heroism of the women of the South, such sympathy was more apparent than real and was confined mostly to the upper classes. He began to realize that, since 1850, a million and a half had gone from the English middle class and settled in the North, and that their relatives and friends at home naturally sympathized with that section in the war.

Toward the close of the year 1863, Maury drew up a "Recast of Resolutions, etc." for a Southern sympa-

[2] "History of the United States from the Compromise of 1850" by James Ford Rhodes, IV, 339.

thizer, the Reverend Dr. Tremlett, of London, and for his 2000 parishioners, the purpose of which was the organization of a society to encourage remonstrance against the war. This developed into the "Society for Obtaining the Cessation of Hostilities in America", which was very active during the year 1864. It had its headquarters at 215 Regent Street, London, and numbered among its officers and members many very influential persons. Leaflets and pamphlets were drawn up and distributed, which called upon the participants to bring the strife and bloodshed, the misery and suffering to a close. Many of these petitions were read in the churches of both Ireland and England, and signatures representing several millions of British people were secured. By that time, however, the war had advanced to that stage in which no such petitions could affect the North and only the complete collapse of the Confederacy would bring the struggle to an end.

In addition to this work as a propagandist which was carried on more or less in the open, Maury was also concerned in political intrigues with the Emperor Napoleon and Maximilian of Austria. These matters were veiled in secrecy, of course; and it is difficult to determine, at this late day, the exact extent of Maury's operations. But there is evidence that it was very considerable. Napoleon had succeeded in conquering Mexico, and the crown had been offered to the Archduke Maximilian of Austria. Maury, who in the old days in Washington had had correspondence with this Austrian prince, thought the time opportune to write to him concerning a scheme which he thought might be greatly to the advantage of both Mexico and the Confederacy. The plan was the offer of assistance in the separation of California from the Union and its restoration to Mexico. Maury hoped that, in this way, foreign complications would arise, which would result in European intervention that would bring the war to a close.

At first, the scheme was received with great favor by Maximilian. Meanwhile, Napoleon changed his mind concerning any plan he may have once had for the recognition of the Confederacy and intervention in her behalf, probably because of England's repeated refusals to join with him in any such action. As Bulloch says, "The invitation to build ships in France was given during the period of successful resistance at the South, and of apparent doubt and trepidation at the North. It was withdrawn when force of numbers and immeasurable superiority in war material began to prevail, and when aid and encouragement was most needed by the weaker side. It suited the Imperial policy, and appeared to be consistent with the designs upon Mexico, to extend a clandestine support to the South when the Confederate armies were still strong and exultant".[3] Accordingly, when Maximilian visited the Emperor in Paris to consult in regard to his acceptance of the Mexican throne, he was persuaded by Napoleon to give up his plan of recognizing the Confederacy and entering into intimate relations with that government; and he did not receive Slidell, the Confederate representative, in Paris, as he had fully expected to do. Nothing further came of Maury's plan. Maximilian was proclaimed Emperor of Mexico by a deputation from that country at the Archduke's palace at Mirarmar on the Adriatic, on April 10, 1864; and on the 15th of that month he em-

[3] "The Secret Service of the Confederate States in Europe", James D. Bulloch, II, 62–63.

barked for Vera Cruz, without making any further advances toward the Confederacy.

So much, then, for Maury's endeavors to secure ships of war for the Confederacy, his work as a propagandist, and his political intrigues. But a fourth activity of his remains to be considered. This had to do with experiments with electric mines,—a continuation of that pioneer work in this field which he had commenced in Richmond early in the war. It has often been stated that this was the primary object of his mission to England; but certainly neither his correspondence nor his diary, which was begun at Bowdon on April 27, 1863, not very long after his arrival abroad, bear out this impression. The fact is, that not until after the comparative failure of his other plans and projects did Maury devote much time and attention to these experiments. Then from July, 1864 up to the time of his departure from England the following spring, everything indicates that his mind was absorbed with the electric mine.

It was not the fault of Maury, however, that this weapon was not more quickly developed, and used more effectively in the war. "I saw", he bitterly complained in one of his letters, "that he did spring at least one mine on Farragut's ships (in the Battle of Mobile Bay). It is so strange to me that sensible men will require to see ship after ship blown up before they will have faith in submarine mining. Don't you remember some drawings that cousin John was making for me in the fall or winter of 1861? That was a plan for mining our channel ways, and our authorities have not yet faith in it to make of it a regular organized system of defense". Even as late as November, 1864 he wrote in his diary: "The question may be asked why I do not hasten home with this information and knowledge? Who—for Davis and Mallory are bitter enemies—will believe my report? The importance of a navy and the value of submarine mining were urged upon them by me from the beginning. Moreover, I have written both the Secretary of War and the Secretary of the Navy urging these things, and here I am ordered to lie.   Another thing, since the whole field is so new I can be of more service here in traversing and exhausting it with experiments where mechanical facilities and appliances are so abundant.   I report results as fast as I obtain them and in a manner, as to circumstances and details, so minute that they may be brought into play as well as though I were there.   Finally, I think it best since so it must be".

The results of Maury's experiments in the electric mine while in England are embodied in the following agreement, made April 11, 1865 with an English electrical engineer as agent: "My dear Sir,—My own experiments show that the electrical torpedo or mine has not hitherto been properly appreciated as a means of defense in war. It is as effective for the defense as ironclads and rifled guns are for the attack.   Indeed, such is the progress made in what may be called the new department of military engineering that I feel justified in the opinion that hereafter in all plans for coast, harbor, and river defenses and in all works for the protection of cities and places whether against the attack by armies on land or ships afloat, the electrical torpedo is to play an important part.   It will not only modify and strengthen existing plans but greatly reduce the expense of future systems. These experiments have resulted in some important improvements and contrivances, not to say inventions and discoveries, which have been fully made known to you verbally. The communication was confidential and for the purpose of making you a party interested in bringing the subject into proper notice. It was also verbally agreed that you should undertake to negotiate with certain powers for the adoption of this new system of defense as improved by me and grants made therefor should be shared between us, I receiving one half of the full amount so granted without charge or deduction of any sort.

"The only restrictions placed upon you in this matter are: 1. The enemies of my country are not for any consideration whatever to have the benefits of these improvements. On the contrary, on making them known to others, you are to make them known in confidence and with a clause in the agreement especially providing against publicity and stipulating that the plan shall not be made known to any Yankee or his government. 2. I had already offered to H. I. H. Grand Duke Constantine, as a token of acknowledgment for his great kindness and friendly consideration shown me and mine, when this war broke out, to place all these my discoveries and improvements at his feet and for the use of his government. I have referred him to you as my confidant and friend who is fully prepared to carry out my plans in all their details, or who will explain them in confidence to any person he may appoint. You are to make no charge, therefore, for imparting this information, at his request, and should he or his government think proper to offer me an honorarium, it is not to be shared by you. 3. My friend, Captain M. Jansen of the Dutch Navy who resides at Delft, has assisted me in a part of these experiments. We are as brothers. All that I have done is known to him and he has the authority to use the information acquired for his own government, provided he may be personally benefited thereby. The restriction here is, that should you deem it worth while to bring the subject before the Dutch government you will first confer with Captain Jansen and shape your course accordingly. Should you effect a negotiation there, please turn over to him my share of the Dutch grant. 4. I restrict you also as to Mexico. Leave that to me. Should, however, any negotiation be entered into with that government, I shall refer the authorities to you for the articles such as wire, etc. required.

"Such in substance is our verbal understanding. But as I am about to leave England, it becomes proper, for more reasons than one, that we should make a memorandum of agreement in writing, to the end of making it good in law and binding also upon our heirs and assigns. With this view, this writing is drawn and the following statement is added. The points upon which this system hangs and which give special value to the information imparted to you concerning it are mainly these: 1. A plan for determining by cross bearings when the enemy is in the torpedo field of destruction and for 'making connections' among the torpedo wires in a certain way and by which the concurrence of each of two operators becomes necessary for the explosion of any one or more torpedoes. This plan requires each operator to be so placed or stationed that a line drawn straight from them to the place of the torpedoes may intersect as nearly as practicable at right angles. And it requires the connection to be such that each operator may put his station in or out of circuit at will. When the torpedoes are laid, a range for each station is established for every torpedo or group of torpedoes. When either operator observes an enemy in range with any torpedo, he closes his circuit for that torpedo. If the enemy before getting out of this range should enter the range for any torpedo from the other station, the operator there closes his circuit and discharges the igniting spark. Consequently, if the ranges belong to the same torpedo, its explosion takes place. But if not, there will be no explosion. Hence, here is an artifice by which explosion becomes impossible when the enemy is not in the field of destruction and sure when she is. 2. The Electrical Gauge, a contrivance of my own which you perfectly understand and some of which you have already made; by means of it one of the tests which the igniting fuse has to undergo before it is accepted is applied. By means of it, the operators can telegraph through the fuse to each other without risk to the torpedoes and by which the torpedoes may without detriment to their explosibility be tested daily or as often as required. And thus the operators can at all times make sure that all is right. 3. A plan for planting torpedoes where the water is too deep for them to lie on the bottom and explode with effect, by which they will not interfere with the navigation of the channels and by which, when the enemy makes his appearance, they may by the touch of a key be brought instantly into the required position at the required depth. These contrivances are very simple. They are readily understood from verbal description. They require neither models nor drawings for illustration. You understand them all. They are of little or no value except to governments and, as against these letters of patent are of no use, I have not deemed letters patent desirable. I have every confidence in you and therefore intrust the whole secret to your keeping and discretion. Having thus placed myself in your hands, let us make this agreement binding also upon our heirs and assigns, and to this end I propose that the necessary steps be at once taken. Yours truly, M. F. Maury, Confederate Navy. To Nath. J. Holmes, Esq."

Maury had at this time fully decided to return to the Confederate States in the spring, and was then arranging his affairs in England with that end in view. He hoped to arrive there early enough to make use of his electric mines in the land warfare of the spring campaign. He had recently undergone a surgical operation, and his friends in England were very much opposed to his going home, some of them being of the opinion that by the time he arrived Richmond would have been abandoned and he would have no home to go to. But he conceived it to be his duty to return, as he might be of greater service there than he was abroad.

Before the date he had set for sailing, May 2, Lee had surrendered at Appomattox and Lincoln had been assassinated; still Maury did not change his plans, but sailed on the Royal Mail Steamer *Atrato* with a quantity of insulated wire, copper tanks, magnetic exploders, etc. for Havana with the hope of being able to keep open Galveston or some other port on the coast of Texas.

He had worried a great deal about the members of his family who were in the Confederate service. "My dreams", he wrote in January, 1863, "are nightly of death and mutilation of children and friends". Just four days after this date his son John, who was at Vicksburg on the staff of General Dabney H. Maury, disappeared while reconnoitering the enemy alone, and was never heard of again.[4]   News of this unfortunate event did not reach the father until April 8, 1863, and soon afterwards he wrote as follows on the evils of war: "War is a great scourge, and this has touched you and me and many a good fellow with a heavy hand.   As I look out upon the landscape that lies before my window, and see the men and women working in the fields, and the fields smiling to man's husbandry, when I see no marks of the spoiler, and recognize that each one is safe in his person and secure in his possessions, then it is I see peace, and think of my poor country with a sigh, and, oh, with what reflections.   'Thoughts on thoughts a countless throng', bless your hearts—you and John—for comforting, with so much solicitude and affection, my poor dear wife in her affliction!   Good brothers are you both.   How lovely and beautiful are the memories of my Johnny!   I wonder if all parents think of their dead as I do of mine.   Bless that sleeping boy!   Never did he, in his whole life, do one single act that either displeased or grieved me or his mother.   'He never offended'.   What an epitaph; and how proudly I write it!   But where is the end of this war to find us—where you and yours, me and mine, and where so many that are dear and near to us?   Our charming circle of relations is, I fear, broken up, never, never to be restored on this side of the grave".

[4] Of this son Maury wrote in the family Bible: "Our noble son, John Herndon, went out from Vicksburg, Miss., alive, on the 27th day of January, 1863, to reconnoiter the enemy.   A few hours afterwards his horse was seen without a rider, but nothing was ever heard of him.   From the footprints and other signs and marks on the levee, it is supposed that he was surprised by a scouting-party of the enemy in ambush within our lines and done to death.   Comely in person, lovely in disposition, generous and brave, he loved right and hated wrong.   Precious in the eyes of his parents, he was very dear to our hearts".

His family had been made refugees three different times, and Maury had been much concerned over their needs and probable sufferings. He wrote in the summer of 1864 to Dr. Tremlett from the Duke of Buckingham's palace at Stow, "I had a letter to-day of May 7th from my daughter Nannie, and she says, 'Flour has gone to $100 per barrel—too high for us—but meal is cheaper, thank God!' . . . 'We had for dinner to-day soup made out of nothing, and afterwards a shin. 'Twas good, I tell you; we all dote on shins'. And again, from my little Lucy, 'Ham and mashed potatoes to-day for dinner; and, as it was my birthday (9th May), Mamma said I might eat as much as I wanted'. Here, you see, there is no complaining, but only a gentle lifting of the curtain, which in their devotion and solicitude they have kept so closely drawn before me. With this pitiful picture in my mind's eye, I felt as if I must choke with the sumptuous viands set before me on the Duke's table. Alas, my little innocents!"

So it was with a heavy heart and the future all dark that he and his young son set sail, after an absence of more than two years, for home,—the home which Maury himself was not to see until several more years of exile had been spent in foreign lands.

CHAPTER XIII

WITH MAXIMILIAN IN MEXICO

When Maury reached St. Thomas in the West Indies, about the middle of May, 1865, he learned from the newspapers that the Confederacy had completely collapsed, but he continued his voyage to Havana. From here his son Matthew, Jr. was sent on home to Virginia; while Maury himself waited to consider what was best for him to do—an old man now broken in health and ruined in finances, separated from family and friends, and without home or country.

Though he had saved practically nothing from the wreck of his financial fortunes, caused by the war, yet his sterling honesty would not permit him to sell the torpedo material and appropriate the money, to which he then had as good a right as any other individual. His conduct of the affairs of the Confederacy in England had been marked with this same scrupulous honesty, in the expenditure of nearly $400,000. Before leaving that country, all the vouchers for that sum were turned over to Bulloch, correct to a figure, as attested by the following letter: "Neither can I close this, perhaps my last letter on business matters, without observing that although the custom here would have sanctioned your receiving a large *per centum* in the way of commission on contracts, purchases, and disbursements made by me, yet you constantly set your face against it and never to my certain knowledge received one shilling".

Maury came out of the war, with no money but with a clear conscience. "I left", he wrote his wife, "$30,000 or $40,000 worth of torpedoes, telegraphic wire, etc.

186

MAURY HALL, UNITED STATES NAVAL ACADEMY, NAMED IN HONOR OF MAURY

which I bought for the defense of Richmond. Bulloch paid for them but they were left in Havana at the break-up, subject to my orders. I write by this mail directing that they be turned over to Bulloch. Now they don't belong to him, neither do they to me. But it is quite a relief to get rid of them by transferring them to a man who I am sure will make the most proper use of them. I did not want any of the $10,000 or $20,000 which they will bring, though some one will get it who has no more right to it than I have".

Now that Virginia had laid down her arms, Maury thought it proper to write a formal surrender of his sword. He accordingly sent the following letter to the officer in command of the United States naval forces in the Gulf of Mexico: "In peace as in war I follow the fortunes of my native old state (Virginia). I read in the public prints that she has practically confessed defeat and laid down her arms. In that act mine were grounded also. I am here without command, officially alone, and am bound on matters of private concern abroad. Nevertheless, and as I consider further resistance worse than useless, I deem it proper formally so to confess, and to pledge you in the words of honor that, should I find myself before the final inauguration of peace within the jurisdiction of the United States, to consider myself a prisoner of war, bound by the terms and conditions which have been or may be granted to General Lee and his officers. Be pleased to send your answer through my son (Colonel R. L. Maury), a prisoner of war on parole in Richmond. In the meantime, and until I hear to the contrary, I shall act as though my surrender had been formally accepted on the above-named terms and conditions".

The status of Confederate agents abroad, at the close of the war, was a very precarious one. As Bulloch writes, "The civil as well as the military and naval representatives of the Confederate States abroad were excluded from 'pardon', under the so-called Amnesty Proclamations, which were issued immediately after the war, and none of them could have returned to the United States without the certainty of arrest, imprisonment, or, under the most favorable circumstances, the alternative of taking what has not been inaptly called the 'iron-clad oath' ".[1]

All of Maury's friends were united in advising him not to return to the United States until the feeling in the North should become less hostile. "Do not come home", wrote his daughter, "General Lee told me the other day to tell you not to". It was their opinion that his letter of surrender would not place him under General Lee's parole, because of the association of his name with the fitting out of Confederate privateers, and that he would be arrested immediately upon his arrival. His brother-in-law, Dr. Brodie Herndon, wrote him a long letter, giving him information concerning the family and the future of Virginia, and advised him not to return for the present. "In view of the state of the public mind in the North at present", he wrote, "I think it would be decidedly unsafe for you to return to this country. Your absence abroad in a semi-diplomatic character, your prominence, and the earnest part taken by you in the cause, would make you a decided object of that 'vengeance against leaders' so openly proclaimed and so plainly visible. In time, I hope, these vindictive

[1] "The Secret Service of the Confederate States in Europe" by James D. Bulloch, II, 415.

feelings will subside, and then, and only then, would it be safe and prudent for you to return".

Before any of this advice could reach him, Maury made his decision as to the course he thought would be best for him to pursue. This was to go to Mexico and take service under Maximilian. Even before leaving England, he had considered this as a possible eventuality, and had written to his friend Jansen about the possibilities of a colonization scheme in Mexico. Furthermore, this item in his diary, written while at sea on his way to the West Indies, shows that the plan was then in his mind: "Secession has failed, I fear, and noble old Virginia is about to pass *sub jugum*, all owing to the President who, not being a statesman himself or a judge of one to call statesmen around him, has sacrificed our sons, our fortunes, and country. At least, so I fear. Where I am bound events will determine. I follow the fortunes of Virginia. If she succumbs, I shall expatriate myself, I think. Events alone will decide my course. Hey ho!" Before his arrival in Cuba, he had made up his mind. In a letter to Dr. Tremlett, written off San Domingo, he declared that he expected to go to Mexico to arrange for emigration from Virginia and other Southern states. "If Max. is wise", he continued, "and will encourage my plans I can assist mightily to make firm the foundations of his dynasty."

It was natural that Maury's thoughts should have turned to Maximilian. Before the war, he had sent to the Archduke, then Commander in Chief of the Imperial Royal Austrian Marine, a complete set of his "Sailing Directions"; and it was through Maximilian's hands that the Austrian gold medal of arts and sciences was conferred on him. Two years later (June 6, 1860) he wrote Maury, enclosing the meteorological diary which had been kept on board the *Elizabeth* on a voyage to South America. These marks of the Archduke's favor, together with Maury's more recent correspondence concerning the possible coöperation of the Southern Confederacy and the new Empire of Mexico, fully warranted Maury's confidence in believing that he might not do better at this crisis in his affairs than to go to Mexico and serve under Maximilian.

By the first of May, 1865, Maury had reached Vera Cruz. From here he went to Mexico City and wrote to General de la Peza, Minister of War, offering to demonstrate his electric torpedoes to him confidentially. Soon thereafter he offered his services to Maximilian, and was warmly welcomed by the Emperor and the Empress Carlotta. He at once laid before them his immigration scheme, which was very favorably received. By the first of August, the Emperor had decided to try the plan, and appointed Maury to the office of Imperial Commissioner of Colonization, with a salary of $5000 a year. In addition to this, he was made on September 23 the Director of the Astronomical Observatory.

None of Maury's family was pleased with his going to Mexico, because of the uncertainty of Maximilian's throne, and would have preferred him to return to England or even to go to Russia or Brazil. His friends were of the same opinion. "The people of Virginia", wrote Captain Jansen, "have shown themselves to be as brave as any people ever have been; but courage is coupled, in patriotism, with perseverance in suffering until better times come for Virginia. All who love her for what she has done ought to love her enough to suffer with her and for her sake. If the best people who have made Virginia what she is desert her at this critical moment, it would be like children leaving their mother in distress. There is no virtue without sacrifice, and, if the Virginians possess the virtue of patriotism, they ought to bring her now the sacrifice of pride. Don't emigrate! Stand by your country with stern courage; learn the patience to bear without shame and with all the dignity of self-command. . . . I don't think you can now return to Virginia; but in three or four years great changes will take place in opinions, and you nor your family won't find a country which would be able to give you anything like her sympathy, or to take Virginia out of your hearts and souls. You ought to go back to your dear state as soon as you can do so safely; and if you had followed my advice you would never have left England, but would have asked Madame Maury to join you there. After a long journey and great inconveniences, perhaps suffering in your health and mind, you'll come back without gaining anything but a sad experience". A month later the same friend wrote, "As long as Max. tries to make what is called a civilized government, his position is unstable and I should not like you to stay there, how sweet and pleasant it may be in the shade of an Emperor's crown. But if he starts on an Eastern policy and succeeds, you may run the chance as his prime minister to become a prince of the empire, or to be hung or shot or something worse".

General Lee also advised Maury against his Mexican scheme. "We have certainly not", he declared, "found our form of government all that was anticipated by its original founders; but this may be partly our fault in expecting too much, and partly due to the absence of virtue in the people. As long as virtue was dominant in the Republic, so long was the happiness of the people secure. I cannot, however, despair of it yet; I look forward to better days, and trust that time and experience—the great teachers of men under the guidance of our ever-merciful God—may save us from destruction, and restore to us the bright hopes and prospects of the past. The thought of abandoning the country, and all that must be left in it, is abhorrent to my feelings, and I prefer to struggle for its restoration, and share its fate rather than to give up all as lost. I have a great admiration for Mexico: the salubrity of its climate, the fertility of its soil, and the magnificence of its scenery, possess for me great charms; but I still look with delight upon the mountains of my native state. To remove our people to a portion of Mexico which would be favorable to them would be a work of much difficulty. Did they possess the means, and could the system of apprenticeship you suggest be established, the United States government would, I think, certainly interfere; and, under the circumstances, there would be difficulty in persuading the free men to emigrate. Those citizens who can leave the country, and others who may be compelled to do so, will reap the fruits of your considerate labors; but I shall be very sorry if your presence will be lost to Virginia. She has now sore need of all her sons, and can ill afford to lose you. I am very much obliged to you for all you have done for us, and hope your labors in the future may be as efficacious as in the past, and that your separation from us may not be permanent. Wishing you every prosperity and happiness, I am, Most truly yours, R. E. Lee".

Unfortunately, this advice from his friends did not

reach Maury until after he had committed himself to the scheme. He was not the type of man who might have sat with hands folded in Havana, waiting for some one to offer him a position. Knowing that it would not be wise for him to return to Virginia at that time, and feeling the responsibility of having a family dependent upon him for support, he pursued the course which seemed to him wisest under the circumstances. If he had been in Virginia at the close of the war, and had been in immediate touch with the situation there and known the attitude of the people toward their future prospects, he would almost certainly have been in agreement with the views of General Lee, and other friends and relatives.

Maury, accordingly went forward with his plan, the main features of which are embodied in the following decree which Maximilian issued on September 5, 1865: "We, Maximilian, Emperor of Mexico, in consideration of the sparseness of the population in the Mexican territory, in proportion to its extent, desiring to give to immigrants all possible security for property and liberty and having heard the opinion of our Board of Colonization, do decree as follows:

Article 1. Mexico is open to immigrants of all nations.

Article 2. Immigration agents shall be appointed, whose duty it will be to protect the arrival of immigrants, install them on the lands assigned them, and assist them in every possible way in establishing themselves. These agents will receive the orders of the Imperial Commissioner of Immigration, especially appointed by us, and to whom all the communications relative to immigration shall be addressed.

Article 3. Each immigrant shall receive a duly executed title, incommutable, of landed estate, and a certificate that it is free of mortgage.

Article 4. Such property shall be free from taxes for the first year, and also from duties on transfers of property, but only on the first sale.

Article 5. The immigrants may be naturalized as soon as they shall have established themselves as settlers.

Article 6. Immigrants who may desire to bring laborers with them, or induce them to come in considerable numbers, of any race whatever, are authorized to do so; but those laborers will be subject to special protective regulations.

Article 7. The effects of immigrants, their working and brood animals, seeds, agricultural implements, machines, and working tools, will enter free of customhouse and transit duties.

Article 8. Immigrants are exempted from military service for five years. But they will form a stationary militia for the purpose of protecting their property and neighborhoods.

Article 9. Liberty in the exercise of their respective forms of religious worship is secured to immigrants by the organic law of the Empire.

Article 10. Each of our Ministers is charged with carrying out such parts of this Decree as relate to his department".

Maury prepared a memorandum to accompany the decree, a set of regulations forty-two in number, and some general remarks on the mineral wealth, climate, general geographical features, and agricultural opportunities to be found in Mexico. The immigrants were to be divided into two classes: Class A were those who had lost all in the war, while Class B were those who were not in straitened circumstances. The first class were to receive a free passage to Mexico and fare at the rate of a *real* a mile to certain lands of the public domain which had not as yet been under cultivation, 160 acres to be allotted to a single man and 320 to a man with a family "with pre-emption right to as much more in each case". The other class were to buy lands from the government, which had been more or less under cultivation, and also private haciendas, both at about one dollar per acre.

That Maury enjoyed the utmost confidence and respect of the Emperor and Empress is revealed in this letter referring to his treatment at the palace of Chepultepec: "There were present the Empress, and one of her ladies, four German naval officers, and a Mexican—all were of his household, I believe. It was mail-day for Europe; the Emperor had been busy at the palace writing, he told me, seventeen letters for the steamer. I got there a moment before he did, so he went into the sitting-room which joins the Empress's chamber. He opened her chamber-door and said, 'Carlotta, here's Mr. Maury'. She came out immediately and commanded me to be seated, the Emperor and the other gentlemen standing. Presently her lady-in-waiting came in; I rose, but she touched me gently on the arm and said, 'The Emperor wishes you always to be seated'. The lady stood also. In a few minutes dinner was announced. The Emperor led off, and we all followed in single file. As I passed through the door, one of the aids—a baron—whispered in may ear, 'On the Emperor's left'. The dinner—excepting the wines, the number of servants, and the liveries—reminded me very much of those Lucy Ellen (Mrs. Maury's sister-in-law) used to give us in our summer visits to Fredericksburg.

"After dinner—say three-quarters of an hour—we, the gentlemen, led by the Emperor, went into the smoking-room. Gilt cigars were handed round; the Emperor did not smoke. Here he drew an armchair up into the corner, and seated me again, he and the others standing until their cigars were nearly finished. Then he took a seat, and commanded the others to be seated. Dispatches were handed him, some of which he handed to me to look into. Presently he dismissed the gentlemen, and said, 'Mr. Maury, you have something to say to me?' 'Yes, sire; I can't manage immigration through the Ministers. I must transact business with you directly, and not through them; nor must they have anything to do with it'. 'That's what I intend', said he". A short time afterwards colonization was placed entirely in Maury's hands and unlimited power to draw on the treasury was also intrusted to him; this indeed was a mark of great confidence.

During the latter part of October, Maury's son Richard with his wife and young son came to Mexico to assist his father and also to prepare himself to take over the work in his absence, for Maury was then planning to make a visit to England to meet his wife and his four younger children. Mrs. Maury had been unwilling to come to Mexico,—indeed to leave Virginia at all; but she at last consented to go to England where the children might enjoy better educational advantages. Maury and his son worked along energetically on the immigration project, but he had already begun to have his doubts as to its success. This feeling of uncertainty was caused, not by the lack of immigrants but by the unreadiness of the Mexican government. It was not prepared to offer them lands on any terms, and many first-rate men from various parts of the South, who had been looking for homes, had gone away in disgust. The fundamental reason for failure should not, indeed, be laid at Maury's feet. But by this time the instability of the Mexican throne had begun to betray itself in the slowness of action and the lack of decision of the Emperor. "The indecision and weakness of Maximilian", writes Stevenson, "prevented his taking full advantage of the opportunity then offered to strengthen the empire. The delay caused by a vacillating policy discouraged the would-be colonists, and before long the flood of immigration was checked".[2]

Still some progress contined to be made. On Maury's recommendation, General Magruder, formerly of the Confederate States army, was placed in charge of the land office, under whom was to be a large number of surveyors, most of whom were former Confederates. Among the other prominent men who had come to Mexico in the summer of 1865 were: Generals Kirby Smith, Shelby, Slaughter, Walker, and Terrell of Texas; Governor Price of Missouri; Ex-Governor Isham G. Harris and General Wilcox of Tennessee; General Hindman of Arkansas; Governor Reynolds of Georgia; Judge John Perkins, Colonel Denis, and Pierre Soulé of Louisiana; and Major Mordecai of North Carolina. Across the frontier had been brought horses, artillery, and everything that could be transported. Both large and small bands of Confederate soldiers had come over into Mexico, and some 2000 citizens had left the United States with the intention of colonizing Sonora in North-

[2] "Maximilian in Mexico" by Sara Y. Stevenson, p. 174.

ern Mexico, though Maury had no connection with this undertaking.

He did, however, send General Price, Judge Perkins, and Governor Harris as a commission to examine lands near Cordoba in the state of Vera Cruz. They handed in a very favorable report, and here a colony, named the "Corlotta" in honor of the Empress, was planted. Of its prospects Maury wrote enthusiastically: "In the olden times Cordoba was the garden spot of New Spain. There stands on one side, and but a little way off, the Peak of Orizaba, with its cap of everlasting snow, and on the other the sea in full view. These lands are heavily in debt to the Church, and as the Church property has been confiscated—not by the Emperor, though—Max. took possession of these lands for colonization. The railway hence to Vera Cruz passes right through them; and I am now selling these lands to immigrants, as fast as they can be surveyed, at $1.00 the acre on five years' credit. There are about forty of our people already there. Perkins has bought himself a house and has sent for his family; so has Shelby, and so have a number of others. Mr. Holeman of Missouri, an Episcopal clergyman, with his family—nice people—has been engaged by the settlement as pastor and teacher. I am going to reserve land for a church, cemetery, and school-house. Thus you see, my sweet wife, colonization is a fact, not a chimera. By the time these lands are paid for they will be worth, even if no more settlers come to the Empire, $20, $30, or even $100 the acre, for they produce everything under the sun, and yield perpetual harvests".

Maury's son Richard secured 640 acres of land in this colony; and by the first of the year 1866 about thirty families had been located there. Other colonies had been established by that time in Chihuahua by Bryant of Arkansas, on Rio Verde in San Luis Potosi by Mitchell of Missouri, and in Jalisco by Terrell of Texas. Furthermore, the last of February, 1866, two ship loads of immigrants, who had been refused permission by General Sheridan to embark from New Orleans, arrived at Vera Cruz by way of Havana. This was the condition of immigration when Maury left Mexico for a visit with his family in England.

Tentative permission for such a visit had been granted in September of the preceding year, and early in the following year Maximilian graciously made good his promise in the following letter: "My dear Counselor Maury,—I have the pleasure of answering your kind letter of the 22nd of January in which you express your just desire to see your family again. If on the one hand I behold with regret your absence for some time from the Capital where you are so effectively helping us with your intelligence; on the other hand, I realize that it is quite necessary to fulfill one's most sacred duties toward one's family, and in consideration of this I cannot oppose your voyage, and my only wish is that you carry it out successfully and that you return with your family. I hope furthermore on returning from my journey to Cuernavaca to see you in Mexico (City) before you undertake yours, in order to take leave of you in person. Your most affectionate, Maximilian".

This letter was accompanied by one from the Empress, as follows:

"My dear Sir,—I have spoken to the Emperor respecting our conversation of Friday last, and he wishes me to tell you first, that he grants you a complete leave of absence to arrange your affairs in England and allows you to set off by the next French packet, but that if he returns to Mexico in the meantime, he hopes yet to have the pleasure of seeing you; secondly, that he quite agrees with your purchasing the instruments for studying the rainy season; and thirdly, that he approves of any effort you may make to introduce the cinchona tree, and authorizes you to have sent from Kew a few specimens of this valuable plant. Hoping to have fulfilled my errand to your satisfaction, I only want to renew my best wishes for your voyage and successful exertions in England, whilst I remain, Yours sincerely, Charlotte".

Here it should be said that, in the matter of cinchona cultivation, Maury left a lasting blessing to Mexico. Before leaving England in 1865, he had discussed the possibility of the introduction of this febrifuge-yielding tree into certain mountainous districts of Mexico, with Mr. Clements Markham, who had established the cinchona plantations in India and was then in charge of all matters relating to them in the India Office. The feasibility of such an introduction of the plant having been agreed to, Maury on his return to England secured three packets of seeds from Markham, which were sent to Mexico, and from them successful plantations were established near Cordoba and in other sections of the country. Thus Maury left a living monument to himself in the country of his adoption and short residence.

Though the letters of both the Emperor and the Empress indicate an expectation of Maury's return to Mexico, yet in a letter to his wife, written before his departure, he leaves the impression that conditions in that country might not render this advisable. It was also understood by some of his friends in the United

States that he was going to England to assist in the laying of a telegraph cable from England to the West Indies and Mexico, and his son Richard thought his father would not return if the cable succeeded. Though Maury did not become connected with this enterprise, yet there developed in Mexico very soon after his departure conditions which made his return inadvisable. In fact, events in that unhappy country were fast moving toward Maximilian's tragic end; and Maury was destined never to see that country nor its unfortunate rulers again.

CHAPTER XIV

Reunited with His Family in England

Maury arrived in England from Mexico, on March 29, 1866, and was once more united with his wife and younger children in London, at No. 30 Harley Street. His appearance had been so completely changed by the sorrows, hardships, and anxieties of the long years of separation that none of his children knew him. Indeed, his youngest daughter, on seeing him for the first time after his arrival, exclaimed, "This is not my papa! This is an old man with a white beard!"

As soon as Maury had departed from Mexico, those who were jealous of him and hostile to the Empire and Maximilian brought pressure to bear which resulted in the abolishing of the immigration scheme. This was made known to Maury through the following letter from the Emperor: "My dear M. F. Maury,—Impelled by motives of economy and convenience to abolish the Imperial Commission of Colonization which in the month of September of last year I confided to your loyalty and superior knowledge, I must on informing you of this measure express the pleasure and satisfaction I feel for the exertions you have so successfully made in the Empire to augment its population, without which the various sources of wealth contained in its fruitful soil cannot be made productive. If your talents cannot for the present be made available in that way, I am convinced that they will be eminently useful in the direction of the Observatory which situation I formerly conferred on you, and in which I trust you will continue, that our

Maury and His Family Reunited in London in 1868 After His Return from Mexico. (*See reverse.*)

Mrs. J. R. Werth of Richmond, Virginia, a daughter of Maury (Mary Herndon Maury in the photograph) has kindly identified the group as follows: beginning with the lady standing on reader's left, Eliza Hull Maury, daughter; Admiral M. H. Jansen, Netherlands Navy, a warm friend of the family; Lucy Minor Maury, daughter; Mary Herndon Maury, daughter; Matthew Fontaine Maury, Junior, son; Mrs. Diana Fontaine Maury Corbin, daughter. Commodore Maury is seated holding his granddaughter, Nannie Maury Corbin, while Mrs. Matthew Fontaine Maury is seated to reader's right. Date of picture, 1868.

beautiful firmament examined by your intelligent eye may procure us the means of profiting by the knowledge which science has already acquired, and of making even new discoveries to increase the fame which you have already so justly attained. Whenever circumstances will permit a new development of colonization, I intend making appeal to your advice and activity and I will now direct the necessary localities to be prepared in the Palace for the Observatory in order to be able to have you always near me. Believe me, Your affectionate, Maximilian".

This letter probably occasioned no very great surprise to Maúry, but he waited several weeks after receiving it before he replied, in part, as follows: "I read, in your letter of April 19th, fresh proofs of your Majesty's confidence and friendly consideration; I am touched by them. I am grieved to learn that your Majesty should be compassed with difficulties so serious as must be those which made it necessary to abandon such a cherished policy as I know that of colonization to have been. . . . Colonization being suspended, I fear that my return to Mexico would tend rather to increase the embarrassments than to smooth any of the difficulties by which your Majesty is surrounded. This fear, my solicitude for the welfare of the Empress and yourself, and the deep concern I feel for your success in one of the noblest undertakings that ever animated the human breast, make me pause. . . . In stating the conclusion, I hope I may not be considered unmindful of obligations or insensible to kindness. Far from it. Proof that I recognize both in their highest sense is found in the fact that in homage to them I forego the high and honorable position so kindly offered me near the person of your Majesty in the service of your Empire. . . . That God may ever have your Majesties in His holy keeping is the constant prayer of your earnest well-wisher and humble friend, M. F. Maury". Thus came to an end Maury's attempt to found a "New Virginia" in Mexico.

Having declined Maximilian's invitation to continue in his service, Maury began to cast about for some other way of earning money to support his family. The first thing that suggested itself to his mind was to make use of his new discoveries in the electric mine. Though the English engineer Holmes had carefully guarded the secrets embodied in these new ideas which had been intrusted to him by Maury, yet he had done nothing in their exploitation and a clear field was thus left for Maury to attempt to secure their adoption by the various European governments. He accordingly conceived the idea of opening a sort of school for instructing any representatives that foreign countries might send to him, for the fee of 500 pounds per country. This offer was made by him through a circular, which he sent out April 25, 1866 to various diplomats in London, recommending three representatives from each country. He was almost immediately invited by the French government to come to Paris to teach its representatives, for which instruction the sum of 25,000 francs was to be paid. Maury accepted this offer, and in the course of his lectures, given on May 21 and 28, 1866, he demonstrated the effectiveness of his electric mines on the River Seine at Saint Cloud in the presence of the Emperor Napoleon. This visit led to his being invited to become a French citizen, and his being offered a position in the Meteorological Observatory in Paris. His family was not willing for him to accept this position but preferred to return to the United States at the earliest opportunity, and he accordingly declined the offer.

In July, 1866 representatives from Sweden and Norway, and Holland came to London to be instructed. There is some evidence that Russia and England also sent representatives at this time. "I have a school under weigh", humorously wrote Maury, "with Sweden and Norway as pupils—board and tuition 500 pounds. They will graduate in 'sea mining' this week. Monday the 16th, the school opens for the Dutch at 500 pounds. I have heard no more about turning Frenchman. But the King of Wurttemberg has been pestering me to keep the Prussians out of his pea-patch of a kingdom. 'Barkis is willing', but I can't say whether anything will come out of it; I think not as the war looks like it is drawing to a close".

The lectures which Maury gave in connection with the demonstrations of his mines gave an introductory sketch of all that his predecessors since the time of Priestly had done in this field, an account of all that had been accomplished by the South with this new weapon during the late war, and then in detail the results of his own experiments. As far as the submarine mine was concerned, he added nothing new to what he had set down in the agreement with Holmes which was drawn up by him just before leaving England near the close of the war. But as to their use on land, the following details appear for the first time among his papers: "After this hasty sketch, I come to electrical torpedoes for guarding mountain passes and roadways, etc., for the protection of strongholds and the defense of fortified positions. Shells cast for the purpose should be used, but in an emergency tin canisters, or any other perfectly water-tight cases, will answer. I am not aware that electricity was used by either of the belligerents in the late American war for springing mines on land.

"The cases for land-torpedoes should be shells cast expressly for the purpose. The thickness of the shell being from one-fourth to an inch, and even more, or less, according to the size and the probable handling in transportation.

"They should be spherical; only instead of a hole for the fuse, as in a hollow shot, they should have a neck like a bottle, with a cap to screw over—not in—the neck. The case should be charged through the neck, and the wires let in through two holes, counter-sunk, diametrically opposite, the counter-sinking being for the purpose of receiving pitch or other resinous matter to keep the water out. The fuse, being adjusted to the wires, should be held in its place by a string through the neck, while the wires are drawn out taut and sealed within and without. Having proved the fuse, first fill and then drive in a wooden peg. Then fill the space between it and the screw-cap with red lead, and screw down tight so as to make it water-tight. Now secure the tails of the wires so that they will not be chafed or bruised, and the mine is ready to be packed for transportation. They are generally to be used in stone fougasses, the wire being buried at convenient depths, and all marks of fougasses and trenches removed as completely as possible. Any number, not exceeding twenty-five or thirty, may be arranged in a single circuit for the ebonite; but if the magnetic exploder of Wheatstone be preferred, and the ground be perfectly dry, hundreds may be planted in a ladder-circuit, which you have seen handled.

"The operator may be at any distance from these

mines when he explodes them, provided only he has established some mark or point which, on being reached by the enemy, should serve as his signal. The area of destruction of one fougasse, properly constructed, with a charge of twenty or twenty-five pounds of powder, may be assumed to be that of a circle seventy-five or eighty yards in diameter. Twenty mines would therefore serve for a mile. Several miles may be planted in a night, and the assailants may be enticed or invited out in the morning. Passes before an invading army may be mined in advance, and thus, if he cannot be destroyed, his progress may be so retarded by dummies or sham mines as almost literally to compel him to dig his way.

"The power to telegraph through these torpedoes is of little consequence, inasmuch as there need be but one station and one operator. Using the testing-fuse manufactured by Abel, and a weak voltaic current, the operator can at any time satisfy himself as to continuity. Thus bridges and gulfs or breaks are not required for the land as they are in sea-mining. Ebonite has the further advantage on land that it takes but a single wire.

"Forts may be protected against assault, and your own rifle-pits from occupation by an enemy, simply by a proper distribution of those new engines of war. They may be planted line within line, and one row above another, and so arranged that volcanoes may be sprung at will under the feet of assaulting columns.

"The only attempt that was made in the late American war to bring the electrical torpedo into play on the land was made by the Confederates at Fort Fisher, in 1865, just before its fall. The narrow landspit over which the attacking party had to advance was mined. The officer in charge used the magneto exploder. But the mines

would not go off, owing no doubt to defective arrange-
ment, for the instrument was new to him, and he had not
been posted up as to the virtues of the ladder-circuit.
The instrument used on this occasion was just such a
one as this before you. It was the first that had reached
the Confederacy. Here is then a most striking illustration of the importance of previous study and drill in
this new and important arm of defense".

In addition to Wurttemberg, Maury offered this instruction in electric mining to her enemy Prussia, and
also to the Governor General of Canada for the sum of
1000 pounds sterling. These offers were not accepted.
His experiments had, however, been made known in this
way to a number of different governments, later information concerning his discoveries leaked out through
his agent in London to other countries, and finally his
system became so generally known that his particular
contributions to the development of this weapon of warfare were lost sight of, and as a consequence Maury has
not been given the credit that is justly due him in his-
tories of the electric mine.

The money which Maury received from these demonstrations of mines came at a time when it was greatly
needed, for he had lost practically all his property in the
United States through the war and after his last arrival
in England he had had the further misfortune to lose,
through the failure of a banker, all he had brought from
Mexico. At about this time, however, assistance came
to him from another source. Indeed, before his departure from England near the end of the war, a "Maury
Testimonial" had been begun at the instigation of some
of his English friends, especially the Reverend Dr.
Tremlett, and by Commodore Jansen. While Maury

was in Mexico, these friends solicited funds for him both in England and on the Continent, Tremlett even taking the trouble of traveling through Sweden, Denmark, and Russia for that purpose. A few months after Maury's return to England this sum had reached the total of 3000 guineas. Holland contributed 1100 pounds, the Grand Duke Constantine gave privately 1000 pounds, and naval officers, scientists, and friends of Maury in England and elsewhere on the Continent subscribed the remainder.

The presentation was made at a special dinner given in Maury's honor at Willis's Rooms in London on June 5, 1866. Sir John Pakington, First Lord of the Admiralty, presided, and there were present the Danish, Mexican, and Argentine ministers, six British admirals, high officers of the Swedish and Russian navies, General Beauregard of the Confederate army, Professor Tyndall, and many of Maury's personal friends like John Laird, Commodore Jansen, and Dr. Tremlett, who was Honorary Secretary of the Testimonial Fund. The purse containing the 3000 guineas was presented in a handsome silver-gilt casket, and was accompanied by the following testimonial: "We the undersigned beg your acceptance of the accompanying purse of Three Thousand Guineas in appreciation and acknowledgment of the eminent and disinterested services which through years of untiring zeal in the cause of science you have rendered to the maritime nations of the world. Receive from us this public testimony of our regard with every wish for your future welfare and happiness".[1]

[1] In 1888 Norway, through Rear Admiral Neils Ihlen, Royal Norwegian Navy, sent to Maury's children the sum of $2180.74 which had been intended to be applied to the Testimonial Fund.

In July, 1866, Maury was engaged by Richardson and Company, a publishing house of New York City, to write a series of geographies for the public schools. It was agreed to make the series embrace "First Lessons in Geography", "Intermediate Geography", "Manual of Geography", "Academic Geography", and "Physical Geography". Maury was to be paid $10,000, $1000 for each volume on the receipt of the manuscript and $1000 more for each volume three months after publication. He was to receive also $600 for revising each book, for five successive years. The following year an additional agreement was signed for the publishing of "Practical Astronomy for Schools", Maury to receive $1500 after the delivery of the manuscript and $1500 three months after its publication.

In August, 1866 Maury wrote, "I am hard at work on Geography No. I, 'Brave' drawing the maps. Well, I could not wind up my career more usefully—and usefulness is both honor and glory—than by helping to shape the character and mould the destinies of the rising generations". Most of the work on these school books was completed before he left England to return to Virginia in the summer of 1868, but at that time only the first two of the series; namely, "First Lessons in Geography" and "The World We Live In", which was the "Intermediate Geography" of the contract, had been published. From the very beginning their reception in the United States was very flattering, and Maury was delighted with his success.

The first little book contained only sixty-two pages. Its preface stated that the pupils were to be taken on imaginary voyages and journeys twice around the world —once by sea and once by land, and it closed with these very significant words: "The teacher should *teach*, as well as *hear recitations*". The second book had just one hundred pages, and was published the same year. These two books were later merged into one, which was entitled "Elementary Geography", and afterwards called "New Elements of Geography". In the preface of the 1922 edition of the latter is the following tribute to Maury's ideas of pedagogy: "Maury refused to follow the plan of all accepted textbooks of that day. His plan was to present, in simple words and in the form of a story, interesting facts about the different peoples of the earth, their homes, their industries, and the lands where they live; and at the same time to call attention to those physical laws which largely determine the condition, the character, and the industries of a people. . . . When published, these geographies were such a radical departure from the old methods that many teachers were not prepared to accept them; but leading educators have gradually come to Maury's position, and to-day the principles that he advocated are endorsed by the Committee of Fifteen of the National Educational Association". The account of the other books in Maury's geographical series, which were not published until after his return to Virginia, will be found in the next chapter.

When Maury left Mexico he had some hope of becoming connected with the laying of submarine cables in the Atlantic. But the only opportunity that presented itself was the offer of 1000 pounds for the use of his name in connection with the North Atlantic Cable. Maury was unwilling to agree to this, and the proposition did not materialize. He kept up his interest in such engineering work, however, and in July, 1866 he wrote that he had filed "provisional specifications" for a patent to improve the manufacture and laying of deep-sea cables, which would decrease the cost almost one half. But in the final successful laying of the Atlantic Telegraph Cable, completed in that very same month, Maury had no part. Though Field had been, before the war, quite ready to accord him due credit for his assistance in laying the first cable across the Atlantic, yet at the banquet given him by the New York Chamber of Commerce at the Metropolitan Hotel, on November 15, 1866, he only casually referred to Maury's name. Two years later at a dinner in his honor in Willis's Rooms, London, on July 1, 1868, Field did not even mention, in his speech, the name of Maury, who that very day sailed at last for his home in the United States.

The success of the Atlantic Cable, however, brought Maury another decoration. This was offered by Maximilian in the following letter: "My dear Counselor Maury,—It was with pride that I heard of the scientific triumph just achieved, and due to your illustrious labors. The Transatlantic Cable, while uniting both hemispheres, will continually recall to their minds the debt of gratitude they owe to your genius. I congratulate you with all my heart, and I am pleased at announcing to you that I have appointed you Grand Cross of the Order of Guadalupe. Receive the assurance of the good wishes of your affectionate, Maximilian". Maury, not realizing perhaps that Maximilian recognized justly his right to share in the honor of the final success of the laying of the Atlantic Telegraph, replied modestly, "The letters of the 16th and 18th of August with which I am honored show how kind and good your Majesty always is. They do me much—too much honor, for I had no hand in the achievement to which your Majesty so graciously refers. The Telegraphic Cable in which I am to take part is not yet ready; when it is, I hope to deserve the Imperial 'well done' which is ever ready to encourage all good works. For the present, therefore, I do not ask for the decoration of Grand Cross of the Order of Guadalupe".

In the same letter, Maury shows that he was not unmindful of the trend of events in Mexico, for he continued, "Events have vindicated the wisdom of my not returning to Mexico. Jealousies within and enmity without had already paralyzed my efforts to serve your Majesty and Empire. I still see in the efforts of the Emperor and Empress of Mexico to give good government with its blessings to that distracted country one of the most sublime moral spectacles that is to be found in the annals of dynasties. As soon as I discovered that I could not assist in the noble work I resolved to stay away, for I have not the heart either to hinder or embarrass your Majesty in these great labors. Animated by the sentiments which I professed when first we met, I have the honor to subscribe myself an humble but true friend of your Majesty's. M. F. Maury".

By the end of June, 1866, matters had come to such a pass in Mexico, through the exhaustion of the resources of the government, the announced determination of Napoleon III to withdraw all French troops from the country, and the opposition to Maximilian's regime by both republicans and clericals in Mexico as well as by the government of the United States, that the throne appeared so much in danger that the Empress determined, much against Maximilian's wishes, to go to France to make personal appeal for assistance from the Emperor Napoleon, who had promised Maximilian to support him in Mexico for five years. After failing to secure help from the French Emperor who had concluded that it was not politic for him longer to support his protegees in Mexico, she left the palace of Saint Cloud, after exclaiming, "What after all should I, a daughter of a Bourbon, have expected from the word of a Bonaparte!" Going thence to Pope Pius IX in Rome, she was equally unsuccessful in obtaining papal intervention. So terrible was the effect of this failure upon the overwrought Empress that she immediately afterwards, October 1, lost her reason and became hopelessly insane.[2]

Maximilian was informed of his wife's condition, and made up his mind to abdicate the throne. In this he was advised by General Bazaine, through instructions from his master, Napoleon himself, who wished Maximilian to leave with the French troops. But in an evil hour he listened to the advice of the clericals and made up his mind to remain in Mexico. Events then moved rapidly to a tragic climax. The French troops began leaving in February, 1867, the last embarking March 12; the republican government under Juarez extended its power rapidly, and on May 15 at Queretaro Maximilian with his Mexican generals Miramon and Mejia were betrayed by Colonel Lopez to the Juarists and, after a trial by court-martial, were shot on June 19. Of this

[2] The last letter that Maury received from the unfortunate Empress enclosed photographs of herself and Maximilian. After becoming insane, she was taken to the Château de Bouchout in Brabant, Belgium, where she continued to write pathetic love letters to her "dearest Maximilian", whom she did not realize to have been dead. Death came to her at the age of eighty-six, on January 19, 1927. During the World War, a heavy guard was placed around her villa by order of the Kaiser and this placard set up: "This villa is the property of Her Majesty the Empress of Mexico, sister of His Majesty Francis Joseph, Kaiser of Austria. Disturbances in the neighborhood will be punished with the utmost severity".

event Maury wrote, "Poor Max!   He died for his honor. He and 'my' Carlotta are the marytrs of the age".

As affecting his own affairs, he afterwards wrote of this Mexican tragedy, "But for my good luck in having J. D. and Mal. for enemies to send me here into banishment, and then kind Mexican villains to intrigue me out of Mexico, you see the rocks that but for enemies I should have split upon".   A very few years afterwards the mills of the gods ground out their punishment for the faithless Emperor Napoleon, and his empire went down like a house of cards before the onrush of the German armies in 1870.   Of Maury's connection with Maximilian and Napoleon, his cousin Rutson Maury wrote, "It was a special Providence that carried you away from Mexico and that prevented your linking your fortunes with those of Louis Napoleon".

Maury's decision to remain in England turned out better, in every way, than he had anticipated.   Here in London in the midst of most pleasant and congenial surroundings he lived with his wife, three youngest daughters, and son Matthew, Jr., who was then attending the London School of Mines.   During this peaceful life, in 1866, Maury became a regular member of the Church, being confirmed with his son and his daughter Lucy in Dr. Tremlett's church at Belsize Park, London, by Dr. Charles Todd Quintard, Bishop of Tennessee, who was then in England to attend the Pan-Anglican Assembly at Lambeth and also to raise money for the University of the South at Sewanee.

In 1868, Maury was signally honored by Cambridge University which bestowed upon him the degree of LL.D. He was accompanied to Cambridge for the ceremonies by his wife, his daughters Mary and Lucy, and his friend, the Reverend Dr. Tremlett. Maury thus humorously referred to the occasion: "So you don't know what I mean by the 'coronation', eh? Why boy, I'm a Cambridge LL.D. and am going there, I and Max and the Queen on the 28th—she to unveil the Prince Consort and I to be rigged up in 'died garments from Bozra' in a gown and a cap and a beautiful red silk cowl and hear myself all done up in Latin!"

The "Max" whom Maury mentioned in this letter was Max Müller, the famous Sanskrit scholar. Still another distinguished savant received the LL.D. on the same day; this was William Wright, translator of Egyptian manuscripts and hieroglyphics at the British Museum.[8] He wrote afterwards to Maury of the bestowal of the degrees as follows: "I have not been at Cambridge lately, but I know that all our friends there are well. Max Müller is now in Germany; I hope to see him at Kiel at the end of September, when we shall both attend the gathering of the German Orientalists. Lord, what a figure we three of us looked, dressed up like *lobsters*, in the midst of that big hall, gazed at by such a host of people, 'when shall we three meet again?' Certainly never under the like circumstances. I was glad to see that Oxford conferred its degree the other day on your poet Longfellow".

During the ceremonies, the Dean made a long oration in Latin, which was addressed to the newly-made

---

[8] It has often been stated that the poet Tennyson received the LL.D. from Cambridge at this same time. This is incorrect. A letter of May 12, 1926, from the Registrary of Cambridge University states that on May 28, 1868, the "Degree of LL.D. *honoris causa* was conferred upon: Frederick Max Müller, Professor of Comparative Philology, Oxford; William Wright, Assistant in the Department of MSS., British Museum; and Matthew Fontaine Maury of Virginia".

"learned Doctors". The portion of this which introduced Maury is as follows: "I present to you Matthew Fontaine Maury, who while serving in the American Navy did not permit the clear edge of his mind to be dulled, or his ardor for study to be dissipated, by the variety of his professional labors, or by his continual change of place, but who, by the attentive observations of the course of the winds, the climate, the currents of the seas and oceans, acquired these materials for knowledge, which afterwards in leisure, while he presided over the Observatory at Washington, he systematized in charts and in a book—charts which are now in the hands of all seamen, and a book which has carried the fame of its author into the most distant countries of the earth. Nor is he merely a high authority in nautical science. He is also a pattern of noble manners and good morals, because in the guidance of his own life he has always shown himself a brave and good man. When that cruel Civil War in America was imminent, this man did not hesitate to leave home and friends, a place of high honor and an office singularly adapted to his genius—to throw away, in one word, all the goods and gifts of fortune— that he might defend and sustain the cause which seemed to him the just one. 'The victorious cause pleased the gods', and now perhaps, as victorious causes will do, it pleases the majority of men, and yet no one can withhold his admiration from the man who, though numbered among the vanquished, held his faith pure and unblemished even at the price of poverty and exile".

Thus did England make amends for its former failure to honor Maury before the Civil War when medals and decorations were bestowed upon him by so many other European governments. While in Cambridge, Maury gave a lecture on "Science and the Bible; Educational Ideals of the South" to further the interest in England in the financial support of the University of the South at Sewanee, Tennessee. In this address he contended for religious education in the college, and maintained that the Bible and science do not conflict if each is rightly interpreted.

Not long after Maury's return to England, his friends began to urge him to return to the United States. There was some talk of a professorship in astronomy for him at the University of Virginia; and a definite offer of a chair in the Virginia Military Institute was made to him by the Superintendent as early as February, 1867. A little later he was asked to become the vice-chancellor of the University of the South, and for several months he was favorably inclined toward accepting this position. He finally decided, however, in favor of the professorship at the Virginia Military Institute at $2000 a year. He did not go to Sewanee, he said, because he thought the Episcopalians at the North were not disposed to assist the institution and the financial arrangements did not give the assurance of reasonable grounds for success.

Maury's letter of acceptance of the Chair of Meteorology in Virginia Military Institute is, in part, as follows: "I thank you kindly for your letter of the 3rd inst. (April, 1868), explaining my duties in the new Chair. They being such as therein defined, you have induced me to accept. I should lack courage to undertake a regular course of lectures as one of the faculty, simply because it would lead me into an untried line of life; and as my rule is to put my heart into whatever I attempt to do, and try my best, I should have to work overmuch—especially at the beginning—and I am afraid of that. The consideration, therefore, that I am not to be charged with a class, or expected to deliver a regular course of lectures, removes a 'sea of troubles' and leaves me in a field of research in which I am not altogether a 'raw hand'. . . . You certainly do draw a very bright picture of the work that is before me (The Physical Survey of Virginia)—of the results that are expected from it, and of the success that is to attend my labors. We do not weigh in the same balance the force that I can bring to the work. Therefore, as bright as your picture is, I have my fears of what there may be on the other side. 'Still, it's wise and brave to hope the best', and, bringing willing hearts and ready hands to the work, we'll try to rub even the dark side bright, should it be turned towards us".

Though the General Amnesty was not passed until May 22, 1872, and Virginia had not as yet been restored to normal relations with the Union, her passing from Federal military control to home rule taking place from April to November, 1869, still the Northern attitude toward the Confederate leaders had already undergone considerable change, as evidenced by the release of Jefferson Davis under bail of $100,000 in May, 1867. Maury felt sure, therefore, that he would not be molested if he returned to the United States, and accordingly after bidding his many warm friends in England farewell, he set sail with his family from Liverpool, on July 1, 1868, for the home from which he had been absent for six years,—years filled with unusual and trying experiences.

CHAPTER XV

HIS LAST YEARS IN VIRGINIA

Maury arrived at New York on July 16, 1868, and was agreeably surprised at his treatment there. "The custom house authorities", he wrote, "received me with marked consideration and passed all luggage without difficulty". Early in August he reached Richmond, much pleased with his reception in his native state. "In the South", he declared, "it's been a sort of ovation. . . . My coming home to share the hard lot of these people instead of accepting French honors is looked upon as a high display of patriotism".

After spending a part of the summer at the White Sulphur Springs as a guest of the proprietors, he was installed, on the 10th of September, in his professorial chair at Virginia Military Institute. The ceremonies were held in the open air on a temporary platform in front of the Superintendent's quarters. The faculty of Washington College, of which General Robert E. Lee was then the Rector, were present, as well as a large number of the citizens of Lexington. Superintendent Francis H. Smith welcomed Maury on behalf of the Institute, and Governor Letcher, as a representative of the Board of Governors of which he was the president, also made an address of welcome. Maury gave an "extended commentary" on the sciences, as the principal speech of the day. On this occasion, according to one of his daughters, Maury wore his foreign decorations, and "the cadets were mightily pleased and cheered till their little throats were dry".

PORTRAIT TAKEN DURING THE LAST YEARS OF MAURY, WHILE AT THE VIRGINIA MILITARY INSTITUTE

Maury did not take up his residence in Lexington until the following year, on June 10, as his house there was not ready for his family until that time. With Richmond as his home during the autumn and winter, he was busily engaged in lecturing, in making preparations for the physical survey of the material and mineral resources of Virginia, in distributing cinchona seeds which had been sent to him from England, in trying to arouse interest in the establishment of an agricultural school in connection with the Virginia Military Institute, and in working in the interest of the Chesapeake and Ohio Railway and the establishment of a direct line of steamers from Norfolk to Flushing. The most important address that he delivered during this period was given at the Staunton Fair on October 28, 1868. In this speech he referred to the opinion which had gotten abroad in the North, and even in England, that the South had become lacking in energy and enterprise, and he advised that they make use of their water power, encourage German and Dutch immigrants to come to Virginia, and begin to construct better roads.

When Maury went with his family to Lexington to reside, he was greatly pleased with his new home. "Here we are", he wrote, "in our new home, busy fixing up; and things begin to know their places. So we also begin to have a home-feeling. People are very kind, the country is beautiful, the views and the scenery lovely, and both climate and air such that exercise is enjoyment". In these congenial surroundings he set to work with a will in the performance of his new duties, special attention being given to the making of the physical survey of Virginia. The object of this work was twofold; namely, to hasten the development of all the state's natural

resources, agricultural and mineral, and to remove prejudice against the South so that immigrants would be attracted to the deserted farms. As in the old days at the
Observatory, when he was investigating the winds and
currents, Maury brought into play his power of inspiring
others with enthusiastic coöperation, and soon reports
and communications came pouring into his office at the
Institute from all parts of the state. There was some
rivalry, in the matter of the survey, between Washington College and Virginia Military Institute. Maury
declared that the College tried to steal his thunder, and
that he published what was called a "Preliminary
Report" in order to "knock them on the head". The
complete survey was unfinished at the time of his death;
but a portion of it was published by his son Matthew in
1878.

Maury also continued work on his geographical series,
only the first two books of which had been published
before he left England. The "Academic Geography"
of the original plan was abandoned; but in 1871 his
"Manual of Geography" appeared, and in 1873 his
"Physical Geography". The first was very favorably
received. One review dwelt particularly on the author's
power of making a tedious and dry subject interesting
and agreeable, commended the illustrations, and declared that the book would delight any school-room in
which the teacher is not hopelessly unfit to teach.
"We are sure", it continued, "that where it is adopted
the geography lesson will become suddenly and sur-
prisingly popular". The preface to the edition, which
was revised by Mytton Maury and re-copyrighted in
1880 by the University Publishing Company, stated,
"Among the marked excellences of the early edition was

its presentation of geography in the character of a science rather than an assemblage of disconnected facts. Land and air and ocean were treated as parts of a grand mechanism; rivers were discussed not simply as 'divisions of water' but as having definite 'offices' to perform; mountains were not merely masses of a certain altitude, but regulators of rainfall.   It was also carefully pointed out how the geographical position and climate of a country determine its industries.   Trade was shown to be in a special manner under the influence of geographical law".

In a still later revision[1] the publishers called attention to the fact that Maury's text, wherever possible, was retained because it was "so clear, simple, and attractive that it has won for the book the uniform favor of the teachers using it.   The original text makes up so large a part of the book that it is essentially Maury's work. Maury's Geographies never belonged to the old school, but rather to the new.   Being devoted to the study of physical geography, and father of the science of 'Physical Geography of the Sea', he undertook the preparation of his book originally with the intention and purpose 'to redeem the most delightful of subjects from the bondage of dry statistics on the one hand, and on the other, from the drudgery of vague, general ideas' ".

Maury's first book on physical geography was published in London in 1864, while he was in England during the Civil War.   It bore the title, "Physical Geography for Schools and General Readers", and was translated into Dutch, French, and Russian.   The book is said not to have been very popular in England, because it pre-

---

[1] In 1912 it was revised as "Maury's New Complete Geography" and copyrighted by the American Book Company, and is still on the market.

supposed an "extent of knowledge among teachers in schools that seldom exists". Maury accordingly entirely rewrote it for his series; as he says in the preface, it was begun in England in 1866 and was the joint work of him, his wife, and his daughters. This book also was revised after Maury's death, and slightly abridged and re-arranged, though the charm of the author's style was retained. Later, it was revised and largely re-written by Frederic William Simonds of the University of Texas, for the American Book Company, in 1908, though in doing so the attempt was made "to preserve as far as possible the plan of the older work—a plan that has met the approval of a generation of teachers—and at the same time to modernize the text thoroughly".

In 1866, Maury began, under an agreement with his publisher Richardson, another book, entitled "Practical Astronomy for Schools", and this was practically finished before he left England. But the work was never published, though it reached the stage of galley proof, in which condition it has been preserved among Maury's papers. Its failure of publication was probably due to financial embarrassment on the part of the University Publishing Company, which became the firm name of Richardson's company on January 1, 1869. For several years this company had a hard struggle and more than once was on the verge of bankruptcy. Maury experienced difficulty in collecting money due him from the company, and only the advice of his cousin Rutson kept him from resorting to law to force payments.

But all these financial matters were adjusted eventually in an amicable fashion, for the popularity of the geographical series brought in a great deal of money to all concerned. In 1871, Maury wrote that the geographies had already been adopted in more than 5000 schools in the South, with an average of some forty books to each school. A little afterwards he declared that the series had cleared during the year 1871 upwards of $30,000. Finally, on January 1, 1872, he sold all the copyrights to Richardson under the following agreement: "I have sold you the copyright *in this country* to all the books, five in number, and wall maps, eight in the series, and you have paid for them in full. I am to revise and by new editions keep the said five books up to the times, for five years for $1000 in gold a year, counting from January 15, 1870. Two of these annual instalments have become due, for each of which I hold your note. The eight wall maps in place of the fourth school geography originally contracted for, were to be published in my name, but constructed at your expense and under my control so as to justify me in claiming their authorship. Besides this you have generously volunteered to pay me *during my life* ten per cent upon the copy money annually coming to you upon any and all of the books and wall maps aforesaid".

In 1870, Maury was offered the presidency of St. John's College at Annapolis, Maryland, at a salary of $3000 and quarters for his family; but it was declined. He had come to believe that the winters, even of Virginia, were too severe for his health, and spent a portion of the winter of 1870–1871, with one of his daughters and his youngest son, at the home of a sister, Mrs. Halland, at Holly Springs, Mississippi and in New Orleans, Mobile, and Savannah.

Early in 1871, he was urged to become the President of the University of Alabama at a salary of $3500 and home, and with the privilege of selecting his faculty. The proposed salary was raised to $5000, so anxious were the board to have him at the head of the institution, and Maury finally accepted on July 30, 1871 by telegraph, "I will come". But on August 17, he resigned the position on the grounds that the arrangements for funds for the University were unsatisfactory and not in agreement with verbal statements made to him. He had gone so far as to write out his inaugural address and send copies of it to various Southern newspapers, and his "Manual of Geography", which was published at about this time, bore on its title page the statement that he was the President of the University of Alabama.

It was then that Raphael Semmes, famous commander of the *Alabama*, under the impression that Maury was soon to be at the head of the university of his native Alabama, wrote a eulogy of his friend, which appeared in the Montgomery *Advance* of September 25, 1871. It closed with the following estimate of Maury's achievements: "Thou hast revealed to us the secrets of the depths of the ocean, traced its currents, discoursed to us of its storms and its calms, and taught us which of its roads to travel and which to avoid. Every mariner, for countless ages to come, as he takes down his charts to shape his course across the seas, will think of thee! He will think of thee as he casts his lead into the deep sea; he will think of thee as he draws a bucket of water from it to examine its animalculæ; he will think of thee as he sees the storm gathering thick and ominous; he will think of thee as he approaches the calm-belts, and especially the calm-belts of the equator, with its mysterious cloud rings; he will think of thee as he is scudding before the 'brave west winds' of the Southern hemisphere; in short, there is no phenomenon of the sea that will not recall to him thine image. This is the living monument which thou hast constructed for thyself".

Maury had, by this time, become dissatisfied with his situation at Lexington. "I shall not", he wrote, "risk another winter here for two reasons—one on the score of health. The other—I have worked out Physical Survey as far as it can be worked out without money. And I feel that I am not earning my salt. Though the Board of Visitors and Faculty are kind enough to express quite a different opinion. So after the swallows come I shall begin to inquire about lodgings in Fredericksburg or Richmond. In all, except the salt-earning feature, my situation here is as delightful as man can make it". Somewhat later, he declared, "They are sounding me about the University of Tennessee. Remember Alabama; I shall look very closely—and not trust to verbal statements—before I commit myself again. You know I intend to cut out from here at the end of the term anyhow. My situation here is charming and delightful as it can be. And though I may be rendering the state service, the state butters me no parsnips. Virginia Military Institute does that and though V. M. I. tries very kindly to persuade me that it's all the same, I can't see it. And so I am quite ready for Tennessee or anywhere else that will offer inducements sufficient".

He, accordingly, handed in his resignation in May to take effect the following September; but there were so many protests against his action, from the Governor of the state all down the line, that he reconsidered the matter and agreed, in July, to remain at V. M. I. for the time being. After his resignation, he had been approached by a member of the Board of Trustees of the Agricultural College near Blacksburg, Virginia, who asked permission to propose Maury's name as their president, but he declined the proposal. Inquiry was also made of him whether he would accept the presidency of a Polytechnic College to be founded at New Orleans. This appealed to him, particularly on the score of his health, but the project did not materialize.

In addition to his work on the "Physical Survey of Virginia" and his geographical series, Maury spent considerable time upon the preparation and delivery of lectures and addresses, not in great numbers during his first two years at Lexington but with increasing frequency during the last years of his life. Among the notable speeches he made during 1869 were an address to the graduating class of V. M. I., July 2, and another before the Educational Association of V rginia, on December 16. In the former, he emphasized the fact that what they accomplished in life would depend largely on their own 'resolves', that they had not 'finished' their education but merely laid the foundation, that they should desire to master the specialty they took up but not to become narrow-minded, and that they should form the habit of observing nature for there they would see God. In closing, he called upon them to live up to their traditions. The later address is a plea for the giving of more attention in the educational system to the study of the physical sciences in view of the progress and development of physical discoveries; it began with the statement that the study of science should not make atheists, if the subject was rightly interpreted.

Maury often lectured to the students of Virginia Military Institute, though he gave no regular courses of instruction; for example, in 1872 he gave a series of lectures to the cadets on "What We Owe to Science".

The larger number of his addresses were delivered, however, in the interest of the establishment of a system of
universal telegraphic meterological observations and
crop reports,—the plan which he had urged for many
years before the Civil War and which that unhappy
conflict had cut short.   Not long after his return to
Virginia, he began to consider this cherished plan again.
"You remember before the war", he wrote, "how hard I
tried to get up a Telegraphic Meteorological Bureau—
writing and lecturing about it—now as meteorology for
the farmers, now as storm-signals combined with crop
statistics.   When I was in England, during the war, I
proposed to Fitzroy, and after his death to his successor,
Toynbee, a plan for making, by means of an elastic
cloth stretched over his map, a caste of the atmosphere,
so that he might take in his whole field of observation at
a single glance, and so predict with more certainty.
Suppose, for instance, with his map pasted on a table,
he had bored a hole through London, Liverpool, Ports-
mouth, etc., and stuck up in each place a little rod
graduated for the barometer; that his elastic cloth was
then fitted to a slide so that he could set it at the height
of the barometer at each of the stations.   Fancy each
rod to be surmounted by a wind-vane which could be
drawn out or shoved in, to show the force of the wind at
each place.   Thus you would have a 'caste of the atmosphere', and see all about it.   Brooke—'deep-sea lead'
—has suggested just such a plan to Myer (General
Albert James Myer of the Signal Bureau in Washington);
and Myer, I have heard, has adopted it.   The idea, I
think, was as original with Brooke as it was with me".
      The first address which Maury delivered on the plan
for land meteorological observations was at the fair of

the Memphis Agricultural and Mechanical Society, on October 17, 1871. In this speech he said that he had dropped the subject at Brussels because the Royal Society of London had advised against it, but that he had ever since regretted this action because he had learned that all Europe had been with him except Bavaria. He then showed how the machinery for putting the scheme into operation in the United States already existed. "You have your Signal Office", he declared, "where weather reports are continually received by telegraph, and whence telegraphic forecasts are issued daily. . . . You have also the Agricultural Bureau, in the service of which reports embodying many of the facts and observations required are already made, or might be without any additional expense. . . . Do you mean to say that amid all the mind, means, and appliances of the age, the relations between the weather and the crops are past finding out? If I could, with just such a system of researches for the sea, sit down in my office and tell the navigator how he would find the wind, at any season of the year, in any part of the ocean through which he wished to sail, am I promising too much when I tell you that by the plan I now propose the relation between the weather and the crops is as capable of scientific development as were the relations between sea-voyages and the winds twenty-five years ago?" At the close of the address, resolutions were offered that the United States government be petitioned through the State Department in favor of the establishment through international coöperation of a plan of universal telegraphic meteorological observations and crop reports, and that another conference similar to that of Brussels in 1853 be called for that purpose.

The different reaction of two of Maury's friends to this speech is interesting. Rutson Maury wrote, "A large part of your Memphis Address that deals with mercantile matters is sheer nonsense. . . . You ought to have some Sancho Panza to accompany you when you go a-tilting". Being a New Yorker, he would naturally not be in sympathy with an effort to deflect even a small part of its trade from that metropolis. Dr. Tremlett's opinion of the speech was more complimentary. "I have", he wrote, "read your last 'spread eagle' at Memphis. Capital, clever, business-like like everything you do; but unrealizable".

The address was followed up by the sending of resolutions to various state governors, and some attempts were made to gain the coöperation of officials in Washington. In the latter quarter, however, no headway was made, as indicated in the following communication to Maury from Senator Johnston of Virginia: "I therefore called upon Mr. Watts, the Commissioner of Agriculture, who scarcely had the civility to hear me. He made the conversation very short, and said that he had just ordered the meteorological reports which his predecessor had been collecting and publishing to be discontinued. I ventured mildly to suggest that if meteorology did not appertain to his Department, at least Agriculture did. He gave this a qualified assent, but told me very positively that he would have nothing to do with the proposed scheme. I met with the same rebuff in other quarters and fancied that I saw a premeditated and arranged plan of resistance. Under these circumstances it was manifestly useless to move now, and so I have not offered the amendment (to provide funds for delegates to the International Agricultural Congress) and will not do so at this session. I am sorry indeed that a scheme so useful should be so treated".

Maury was undaunted by such rebuffs and continued his campaign. On May 29, 1872 he addressed the National Agricultural Congress at St. Louis, declaring that Europe was ripe for such a scheme and citing the names of the following influential supporters of it abroad: Alexander Buchan, Secretary of the Scottish Meteorological Society; Commodore Jansen of Holland; Quetelet, Astronomer Royal and Perpetual Secretary of the Academy of Sciences of Brussels; Marie Davy, Zurcher, and Margolle, meteorologists and savants of France; and Father Secchi of the Collegio Romano in Italy. The legislatures of Tennessee, Alabama, Mississippi, Missouri, North Carolina, and Virginia, he declared, had passed resolutions instructing Congress to support an international conference; and he suggested that they bring further influence to bear on Congress through state agricultural societies, agricultural journals, and the general press of the country. He called attention to the fact that his interest in the scheme was not a private one, since he had no farm, and could not share in the honor of helping to organize and carry out the plan for the government. He closed with an eloquent plea, emphasizing the benefits to be derived, which he estimated would be as great as those formerly bestowed upon commerce by the results of the Brussels Conference.

On August 13 of the same year he spoke before the Agricultural Convention of Georgia at Griffin. Here he covered about the same ground that he had in his St. Louis speech, and used the same arguments, though the language was different and it was not a mere repetition of the former address.   He also, in it, treated the question of immigration, saying that the prejudice which had arisen abroad against the South must be removed; and he once more touched upon the old problem of better trade communications for that section.   This latter question had been in Maury's mind for years, and he at this time advanced bold and original ideas as to the best means of improving conditions.

He declared in one of his letters to Dr. Tremlett that the seat of empire was fast settling down in the Northwest States.   "They already give the Presidents", he wrote, "and will soon dictate the foreign policy of the country.   They must have a better way to the sea. They have been taught to believe—erroneously—that the best way lies through Canada and the St. Lawrence. It does not; it lies through Virginia.   You will appreciate my feeling on this subject, when I remind you that grain is sent around Cape Horn from California, and delivered at the ports along the Atlantic seaboard at ten cents the bushel cheaper than it can now be sent from Iowa and other Northwest States; that the people throughout these states—and they are the grain-growing states— know that, with a good highway to the Atlantic seaboard, the value of their grain would be enhanced ten, twenty, even thirty cents the bushel; and they think that Canada and the St. Lawrence can give them such a way.   The greatest difficulty in teaching these people that their best way to the sea lies through Virginia, not through Canada, is to get our people to raise funds for the gratuitous circulation of the Reports (Preliminary Report on the Resources of Virginia) in sufficient numbers between this and the next meeting of Congress in December.   If we can do that, the Northwest States will raise their voices in favor of the Virginia route, and demand the money to open it. When that is done, they will not want Canada, and we shall have peace. Thus you see, my friend, I am aiming high and striking far. But with a few heads such as yours to help, we would hit the mark as sure as a gun". Not only in his correspondence, but also in the press as well as in his speeches he continued to advocate direct trade between the South and Europe through the establishment of a Norfolk to Flushing line of steamers, which would turn the tide of immigration toward the Southern States.

On the 18th of September, 1872, Maury spoke to the Farmers' Club of Norfolk, Massachusetts, near Boston. On this occasion, he made a very tactful speech with happy references to his old friend John Quincy Adams, and used only the portions of his previous speeches in favor of meteorological and agricultural observations, that were best adapted to a Northern audience. From here he traveled to St. Louis by way of New York, Niagara Falls (Buffalo), Detroit, and Chicago. On October 9, before the St. Louis Agricultural and Mechanical Association at its annual fair, he spoke as in the year previously on the plan of international coöperation, using the same arguments but adding that at the recent International Congress of Statisticians at St. Petersburg, Russia his scheme had been cheered "by the huzzas of Russians, hochs of Germans, vivas of Latin races, and the hurrahs of the English", and that a special committee had been appointed to further the movement.

Maury was so exhausted, however, by the time he reached St. Louis and was so ill that he could hardly read his address in an audible tone. As a matter of fact, in the summer preceding this lecture tour he had been very ill of the gout and was for a time on crutches. Consequently, when he reached home after spending some two weeks in St. Louis, he was too ill to attend the first annual fair of the Seaboard Agricultural Society, which he was to have addressed at Norfolk, Virginia, on October 23. His address had already been prepared; and as it turned out to be his last, its contents are of peculiar interest. He appealed to the farmers in regard to the necessity of coöperation for self-protection and redress against transportation monopolies and all sources of oppression and discouragement; he contended that domestic commerce should be attended to by Congress as carefully as foreign trade, but that special legislation protected the latter while the former was left to the tender mercies of great corporations; he touched upon his favorite topic of weather observations and crop reports, and many other questions such as tolls and tariffs, the government of railroads, interior water lines and canal projects, the conjunction of the Atlantic and the Mississippi River valley, east and west trunk lines and branches and the ways and means of constructing them without increase of taxation, the regulation of commerce between the states, the naval establishment and wherein it needed reforms, immigration, and labor and capital.

Maury was destined not to live to see the scheme of meteorological observations and crop reports, upon which he had spent so much thought and labor, in operation; but not long after his death a part of his program was carried out when there was an international conference of meteorologists at Vienna in 1873, the United States being represented by General Albert James Myer of the Signal Service of the Army. There are, indeed, those who would deny him any part in the establishment of the present Weather Bureau. On the contrary, there are others who would go to the opposite extreme and give him all the credit for bringing it about. For example, Mr. E. P. Dorr, who was at one time an observer for the Smithsonian and afterwards President of the Board of Lake Underwriters, wrote to Mr. Thompson B. Maury, at that time (1873) in the Signal Office, in Washington that Maury's "intelligent, original mind invented and suggested the present system of meteorological observations; and the writer wishes this in some way to be put upon record, to do justice to the dead Maury, a man whose name and memory will live in all civilized countries on the globe, throughout all time, as an original, great mind. . . . I could not rest unless I told some one that the late M. F. Maury was the originator in design and detail, in all its parts, of the present system of meteorological observations now so generally taken all over the country".

The question of due credit is a perplexing one; but certainly no one could cavil at the modest claim made by Maury's son Matthew in the following letter: "In 1869, Abbé took the question up and began issuing local forecasts from Cincinnati Observatory and out of his success here and efforts in Washington grew the Weather Bureau in November, 1870, with General Myer at its head, to whom belongs the credit of working up all the details and putting the thing on such a practical footing. Till now the Washington work is the admiration of all the world as its daily charts and reports embrace not only the United States but the whole of the northern hemisphere, Australia, and the Cape of Good Hope. Now I think that any calm mind can only say for Father that he had the clearness of foresight to foresee what could be done for the land with the aid of regular stations and the telegraph, but we can't in the smallest degree say that its practical success is due to him. In the future, General Myer will have that credit. Father's reputation must rest on his work at sea and a biography can only speak of other things as indications of his clear and far-seeing mind. The world is full of similar cases in all great improvements, and the world invariably gives the credit not to the man who first thought of them but to the man who puts the ideas into practise".

When Maury was stricken with sickness on his last lecturing tour, he seemed to realize that he would not recover, for when he arrived at home and entered the house he said to his wife, "My dear, I am come home to die". He was immediately helped to his bed, though death did not come until after four long months, during a portion of which time he suffered extreme pain. When not suffering too much, he occupied himself with a revision of his "Physical Geography".

During his long illness, the strength of his Christian faith displayed itself, and he became wholly resigned to the inevitable. Job had always been his favorite book in the Bible; and the 130th Psalm, which he called "De Profundis" and which was sung at Luther's funeral amid the tears of the people, was read to him, at his request, many times during his last days. He was greatly comforted by a week's visit which his brother-in-law, Dr. Brodie S. Herndon of Savannah, made him in the December preceding his death. And towards the end he sent sincere farewell messages to Commodore Jansen in Holland, whom he had loved for many years as a brother, and also to Dr. Tremlett who had brightened with his friendship the desolate years of his exile in England and had influenced him to enter the communion of the Church. A few days before his death he dismissed his physicians, saying, "Don't come to see me any more; leave me to the great Physician".

He derived his greatest consolation and satisfaction from having his family about him, for whom he had always shown throughout his life the tenderest affections of a devoted father and husband. As he talked to them, there would come flashes of his quaint playful humor that had always been so characteristic of him; and he requested that there be no weeping in his presence. He rejoiced in being able to recognize all his family to the end. "You see", said he, "how God has answered my prayers, for I know you every one. . . . I shall retain my senses to the last. God has granted me that as a token of my acceptance. I have set my house in order, my prayers have all been answered, my children are gathered round my bed—and now Lord, what wait I for?" Then he would repeat the prayer which he had composed thirty years before when his leg was broken, and which he had repeated in his daily devotions ever since: "Lord Jesus, thou Son of God and Redeemer of the world, have mercy upon me! Pardon my offenses, and teach me the error of my ways; give me a new heart and a right mind. Teach me and all mine to do Thy will, and in all things to keep Thy law. Teach me also to ask those things necessary for eternal life. Lord, pardon me for all my sins, for Thine is the kingdom and the power and the glory, for ever and ever, Amen".

On the evening before his death, the family sang for him verses from his favorite hymn, "Christ Is Risen", which he called "Pass over Jordan", and also from "How

Firm a Foundation". After the singing he said so that all could hear, "The peace of God which passeth all understanding be with you all—all!" Toward the end he inquired of his son Richard, "Are my feet growing cold? Do I drag my anchors?" Upon receiving an affirmative answer, he said, "All's well". About fifteen minutes before he died, his wife and daughters were requested by him to leave the room, and he was left with his two sons and two sons-in-law. At 12.40 P.M., on Saturday, February 1, 1873, his life came to a close.

The body lay in state in the hall of the Library of Virginia Military Institute from four o'clock in the afternoon of Monday until Wednesday. The gallery round the hall was festooned with black, a large anchor and a cross of evergreens being placed at alternate angles; while the columns were draped spirally. The wall was covered with maps constructed under Maury's supervision, and on opposite sides of the gallery were placed two heavily draped flags, the one being that of his native state Virginia, and the other that of his adopted state Tennessee. In the center of the hall rested the bier, bearing his body, with his breast covered with the foreign orders that had been conferred upon him, and with a gentle smile on his face. Near the bier stood a large globe bearing this appropriate inscription: "The whole world is mourning for Maury".

A funeral service was held in the hall on Wednesday about noon, by the Reverend William Pendleton, D. D. of Grace Church, after which the coffin, attended by the cadet battalion and the faculty of Virginia Military Institute and the professors and students of Washington and Lee University[2] and the citizens of Lexington, was

[2] This was the name given to Washington College in 1871 after the death of General Lee on October 12, 1870.

conveyed to the Gilham vault in the city cemetery, just opposite the tomb of "Stonewall" Jackson. This, however, was only a temporary resting-place. When, shortly before his death, his wife had requested of Maury that she be permitted to bury him in Richmond, he had replied, "Very well, my dear; then let my body remain here until the spring, and when you take me through the Goshen Pass you must pluck the rhododendrons and the mountain-ivy and lay them upon me".

"Home, bear me home, at last", he said,
   "And lay me where your dead are lying;
But not while skies are overspread,
   And mournful wintry winds are sighing!

Wait till the royal march of spring
   Carpets the mountain fastness over—
Till chattering birds are on the wing,
   And buzzing bees are in the clover.

Wait till the laurel bursts its buds,
   And creeping ivy flings its graces
About the lichened rocks—and floods
   Of sunshine fill the shady places.

Then, when the sky, the air, the grass,
   Sweet nature all, is glad and tender—
Then bear me through the Goshen Pass,
   Amid the hush of May-day splendor".[1]

It was the following autumn, however, before Maury's wishes could be carried out. In bearing his remains to Richmond at that time, the family were escorted as far as the river, about a mile from Lexington, by the corps of cadets, the professors of the Institute, and a great many other friends who thus wished to show their love and respect for the great scientist. Some, among whom

[1] The opening stanzas of "Through the Pass" by Margaret J. Preston.

Courtesy of Governor Byrd and of the Virginia State Chamber of Commerce.

MAURY MONUMENT IN THE BEAUTIFUL GOSHEN PASS, ON THE BANK OF THE
NORTH ANNA RIVER, ERECTED BY THE STATE OF VIRGINIA IN 1923

See page 246 and reverse side of this page

The bronze tablet on the monument shown on the opposite side of this page bears the following inscription:

MATTHEW FONTAINE MAURY

Pathfinder of the Seas
The Genius who first Snatched
From Ocean & Atmosphere
The Secret of their Laws.

Born January 14th, 1806
Died at Lexington, Va., February 1st, 1873
Carried through Goshen Pass To His Final
Resting Place in Richmond, Virginia.

Every Mariner
For Countless Ages
As he takes his Chart to Shape
His course across the Seas,
Will think of thee

His Inspiration Holy Writ

Psalms 8 & 107, Verses 8, 23, & 24
Ecclesiastes Chap. 1, Verse 8
A Tribute by his Native State
Virginia
1923

His Last Words
"Carry My Body Through The
Pass When the Rhododendron
is in Bloom."

was Superintendent Francis H. Smith of V. M. I., accompanied the cortege as far as Goshen Pass. In going from Lexington to what was then the nearest station on the Chesapeake and Ohio Railway, one passed through this lovely gorge where the North Anna River forces its way through the mountains some fifteen miles from Lexington. When the cortege reached the Pass, the carriages were stopped and members of the family gathered branches of the rhododendron and laurel and bright yellow maple, and decked the hearse with them, as Maury had requested.

They arrived in Richmond on Saturday, September 27. The burial in Hollywood Cemetery was private, Maury's last resting-place being between the tombs of Ex-Presidents Monroe and Tyler, on a beautiful knoll overlooking the James River. "The lot we have in Hollywood", wrote Maury's son Matthew, "I like particularly because it faces the bright green country and overlooks the rapids of the James River, the sleeper there being always lulled by the murmur of running water, a sound which he so loved to hear". Maury's monument in Hollywood Cemetery bears the following inscription: In Memory of Matthew Fontaine Maury— Born in Spottsylvania Co., Virginia January 14th, 1806 —Died in Lexington, Virginia February 1st, 1873—"All is well", Maury. On another side of the shaft are these words: Entered the Navy of the United States 1825— That of the Confederate States 1861—Author of "Maury's Sailing Directions" and "The Physical Geography of the Sea".

CHAPTER XVI

His Posthumous Reputation

Immediately after Maury's death there was a veritable flood of eulogies of the character and services of the great scientist. They were by no means confined to the colleges, legislators, and newspapers of Virginia; but the scientific journals throughout the world made known in unmistakable terms the high estimation in which he was held. For example, the British journal *Nature* of March 20, 1873, declared that Maury was the first to show how meteorology could be raised to the dignity of a science, and that he was essentially a practical man in the highest sense of the term. "He will certainly", it added, "and deservedly, occupy a niche in the temple of fame as a benefactor of humanity and a promoter of scientific knowledge, to which not many men ever attain". It is difficult to resist the temptation to quote other extracts from the dozens of highly commendatory appraisals of Maury's achievements and character, which appeared soon after his death. But such is unnecessary, if this biography has with a reasonable degree of success given an understandable account of his work and revealed through the assistance of his letters the sterling character of the man.

After this flood of eulogy had subsided, a period of some fifteen years followed during which Maury's name was wrapped in comparative forgetfulness. Then, there appeared in 1888 the "Life of Maury" by his daughter Diana Fontaine Maury Corbin, and the reviews of that volume once again brought his name into the literary and scientific journals where the praises of former years were repeated. The *Athenaeum* of July 21, 1888, after pointing out how Maury's meteorological work had come to be unduly depreciated, declared, "The work (*Physical Geography of the Sea*) remains one of undoubted genius—great if only for the impulse which it gave to the study of this particular branch of physical geography and for the enormous advance in the science of meteorology which we owe to it". The *Saturday Review* of October 20, 1888 said that scientific navigation was almost non-existant before Maury's work and that he had improved the course of every ship on the sea. It would be tedious to quote further from these reviews, and it will be sufficient to state that they were unanimous in their opinion that Maury deserved high rank among the great scientists of the world because of his pioneer work in the field of oceanography.

In this connection, there is a letter which, because of the fame of its author as well as the pertinence of its contents, is of peculiar interest. Thomas Nelson Page, the distinguished Virginia novelist, wrote to Mrs. Matthew Fontaine Maury,[1] on the receipt of a copy of Mrs. Corbin's biography of her father, as follows: "Please accept my thanks for the biography of your distinguished husband which will be an addition to our library both on account of its literary merit and of the information it contains of one of our greatest men. I trust you may live to see the services he rendered mankind suitably commemorated by a monument worthy of him. But whether you do or not, the time will assuredly come when he will be recognized by our people as an honor to the race from which he sprang. I esteem

---

[1] Mrs. Maury survived her husband until the year 1901.

it one of my privileges that in my youth I knew personally two such men as General Lee and your honored
husband".

For many years repeated attempts have been made
to erect such an adequate monument to Maury as the
one mentioned in Page's letter. Immediately after
Maury's death, at the suggestion of Rear Admiral Marin
H. Jansen of Holland, some steps were taken toward the
building of a lighthouse on the Rocas Banks near the
coast of Brazil, as a fitting memorial to the great oceanographer. But the plan did not succeed, as foreign geo-
graphic societies wished the movement to originate in
America, and this country, when approached on the
matter, was found unsympathetic toward the undertaking. The renewed interest in Maury which was
caused by Mrs. Corbin's biography led to an effort in
1890 to induce Congress to appropriate $20,000 to erect
a monument to Maury in Washington; but this attempt
was not successful. Then, the Daughters of the American Revolution began a movement, which lasted for
about fifteen years, to interest the government in
building an appropriate monument in the nature of a
lighthouse upon the Rip-Raps in Hampton Roads, off
Old Point Comfort, Virginia. A final effort was made
to have the memorial built and to arrange for its unveil-
ing during the Jamestown Exposition in 1907; but failure
again met all endeavors.

In 1915 it was suggested by the Superintendent of the
Naval Observatory that a memorial building in Maury's
honor to accommodate the Hydrographic Office and some
of the Observatory activities be erected on the Naval
Observatory grounds, but the suggestion brought no
tangible results. On May 11 of that year, however,

the Matthew Fontaine Maury Association[2] was organized in Richmond, with three specific objects in mind. The first was to have Maury's name placed in the Hall of Fame of New York University. In this they have not as yet succeeded, but in the election of 1925 Maury's name came sixth, with fifty-two out of the one hundred votes cast. The two successful candidates, John Paul Jones and Edwin Booth, received sixty-eight and eighty-five votes respectively; while the other three who were ahead of Maury were John Jay with fifty-nine votes, Samuel Adams with fifty-eight, and "Stonewall" Jackson with fifty-three. The second object of the Maury Association was to induce the State Board of Education of Virginia to appoint January 14th—Maury's birthday —as Maury Day in the schools; this was done June 27, 1916. Their third and most ambitious undertaking was the erection of a bronze statue of Maury in Richmond. In this effort slow but steady progress was made. The Virginia legislature contributed $10,000, and after the close of the World War the United Daughters of the Confederacy gave their support to the raising of funds. The school children of Virginia gave $2000, and many others contributed generously. Accordingly, the sum of $60,000 has now been raised, and the monument will in the near future be put in place at the intersection of Belmont and Monument Avenues in Richmond, where the corner stone was laid with appropriate ceremonies on June 22, 1922. A tentative model of this monument has been made by the sculptor, Mr. F. William Sievers, and approved by the committee in charge of the memo-

[2] Great praise is due Mrs. E. E. Moffitt for founding this Maury Association, and successfully raising the money necessary to build the monument to Maury in Richmond.

rial.   For description of this monument please see foot-
note, end of chapter, page 251.

A long list of minor memorials to Maury have appeared from time to time.   One of the oldest is his
portrait in fresco on the ceiling of the Library of the
State Capitol of Tennessee in Nashville, which was
painted in 1857.   His name, among six or seven others,
adorns the exterior of the building of the Seaman's
Institute, overlooking the Elbe, in Hamburg, Germany;
while the University of Virginia has his name inscribed
on the frieze of its new Rotunda.   There are a number
of other memorials in Maury's native state.   In Lexington at the Virginia Military Institute there is a Maury-
Brooke Hall in which the physical sciences are taught.
In Richmond, the house in which he invented the electric
mine has been marked, and in South Richmond a street,
a cemetery, and an elementary school all bear his name.
Norfolk has a Matthew Fontaine Maury High School;
while Fredericksburg has its Maury Hotel, and has
marked the house where he resided for several years.
In Goshen Pass, a tablet in Maury's honor was unveiled
on June 9, 1923.   The bronze tablet is attached to a
granite shaft about eight feet tall, at the base of which
is to be placed an anchor, weighing 1500 pounds, and 90
feet of chain, of a type used in Maury's time and donated
by the Virginia Pilot Association of Norfolk.   This
memorial, which was designed and constructed by the
sculptor Guiseppe Moretti, was authorized by the
Legislature of Virginia.   In the state of his adoption,
there is only one recent memorial, a tablet in his honor,
placed on the walls of the Public School Building in
Franklin, Tennessee, by the Old Glory Chapter of the
Daughters of the American Revolution.

Courtesy of the Commanding Officer, Commander James B. Glennon, U. S. N.

DESTROYER U. S. S. "MAURY," NAMED IN HONOR OF MAURY

In the United States Navy there has been considerable recognition of Maury since his death,—particularly in recent years. His name is placed at the top of all the charts issued by the Hydrographic Office, in the following phrase: "Founded upon the researches made and the data collected by Lieutenant M. F. Maury, U. S. Navy". In 1918 a destroyer in the U. S. Navy was called the *Maury*, and recently the Secretary of the Navy has named the Naval Oceanographic Research in his honor. At the United States Naval Academy at Annapolis, the left wing of the Academic Building bears the name of Maury Hall. This was originally the navigation wing of the building, and, according to the Superintendent of the Academy (Captain W. F. Fullam, U. S. Navy, in 1915), it was named by his direction "Maury Hall" because of "Maury's distinguished and world-wide reputation in connection with meteorology and the study of ocean currents, etc." In 1919, the United Daughters of the Confederacy established a prize at the Naval Academy, consisting of a pair of marine binoculars, to be known as the "Maury Prize" and to be awarded annually to that midshipman of the First Class who has shown superior excellence in electrical engineering and physics. A portrait of Maury by E. Sophonisba Hergesheimer was presented to the Naval Academy by the Daughters of the Confederacy, Atlanta Chapter, Georgia Division, and unveiled on November 20, 1923.[3]

[3] Of the numerous portraits of Maury, those deserving special mention are in Richmond. There is one by N. H. Busey in the Westmoreland Club of that city, another by John A. Elder in the Virginia State Library, and a third of some merit in Battle Abbey, Richmond. In the State Library is also a cast of the fine bust of Maury made by Edward V. Valentine of Richmond in 1869, which is considered by Mrs. Werth to be a very excellent likeness of her father. There is a statue of Maury over the main entrance to the Meteorological

One of the most recent memorials to Maury is as interesting as it is appropriate. On December 22, 1925, the Martin Vas Isles (Ilhas da Martin Vas) were visited by the Schooner *Blossom* of the South Atlantic Expedition which was sent out by the Cleveland Museum of Natural History for the purpose of collecting specimens from the volcanic islands of the South Atlantic. These islands, individually unnamed and hitherto imperfectly charted, lie about eight hundred miles off the coast of Brazil in the direction of Africa (latitude 20° 31' S., longitude 28° 51' W.). Captain George Finlay Simmons of the *Blossom* and his associates, impressed with the importance of the work done by Maury, decided to give his name to one of the three islands of the group which rises from the ocean like an impressive monument.

All of these memorials, so varied in their nature and so widely distributed, would seem to indicate that Maury's name is by no means likely to be forgotten. Still, his name and his achievements are not so generally known, even in the United States, as they deserve to be. "For myself", wrote Julian Street[4] a few years ago, "I must confess that, until I visited Virginia, I was ignorant of the fact that such a person had existed; nor have Northern schoolboys, to whom I have spoken of Maury, so much as heard his name. Yet there is not one living in the United States or in any civilized country, whose daily life is not affected through the scientific researches and attainments of this man". One is surprised, however, sometimes to find foreign authors more familiar

Station of the German Admiralty in Hamburg, Germany. Recently, the M. F. Maury Chapter of the Children of the American Revolution has been organized at Franklin, Tennessee by Miss Susie Gentry.

[4] In "American Adventures" (1917), pp. 140–145.

with Maury's name, and to meet with references to him where one might least expect any knowledge of his scientific work. For example, in Walter de la Mare's "Memoirs of a Midget" (p. 226), the reader is unexpectedly confronted with this: "I searched Mrs. Bowater's library for views of the sea, but without much reward. So I read over Mr. Bowater's Captain Maury—on the winds and monsoons and tide-rips and hurricanes, freshened up my *Robinson Crusoe*, and dreamed of the Angels with the Vials". Another example, almost equally unexpected is to be found in Vicente Blasco Ibanez's "Mare Nostrum" (p. 65). "He (Ulysses) had learned English", writes Ibanez, "the universal language of the blue dominions, and was refreshing himself with a study of Maury's charts—the sailor's Bible—the patient work of an obscure genius who first snatched from ocean and atmosphere the secret of their laws".

In recent scientific works, however, such as "The Depths of the Sea" by Sir John Murray and Dr. Johan Hjort, "Science of the Sea" edited by G. Herbert Fowler, and "Founders of Oceanography" by Sir William A. Herdman one is not surprised to find full justification for referring to Maury as "The Pathfinder of the Seas", for marine meteorology, they declare, may be said to date from his time. Not only is this title appropriate in that Maury laid out on his charts the best tracks for voyagers to follow on the Seven Seas, but it is also fitting in a figurative sense for he was indeed a pathfinder in the realm of a new science,—the physical geography of the sea. This phrase was, therefore, rightly chosen to be placed on the memorial tablet in Goshen Pass as well as on the one at Franklin, Tennessee, and it is to be prominently inscribed on the monument soon to be erected to

him in Richmond.   This beautifully poetic title, "The
Pathfinder of the Seas", will be his real monument
against which the tooth of time will gnaw in vain, for it
will rest solidly based upon his original contributions to
the science of the world: "The Physical Geography of
the Sea" and the "Wind and Current Charts" with their
"Sailing Directions".

It is not so easy, on the other hand, to describe in a
phrase Maury's personality.   Some of those who knew
him well thought his most characteristic trait was his
modesty; others considered "masculine common sense",
which enabled him to see things in their true light and
their real bearing, most fully characterized him; while
still another declared that he belonged to that class of
men who are *sans peur et sans reproche*.   But his character had too many facets for such a simple characteriza-
tion, and one is forced to turn to a more detailed
summary.   Perhaps, the most nearly satisfying one of
this sort is that written by Francis H. Smith, formerly
Professor of Physics at the University of Virginia and
one who was well acquainted with Maury and his
scientific work.

"Of Maury's personality", Professor Smith wrote, "it
may be said that no one that had the privilege of meeting
him ever forgot the event.   He had the winning manner
and kindly address which seemed to belong to the men of
his race and section.   No worthy young fellow ever felt
ignored or oppressed in his presence. He wore his
honors easily, but while he valued the public tributes he
received, he was not fond of displaying the insignia which
came with them.   He would put on those jewels sometimes in the privacy of home to gratify his children.
He loved the little ones, and if to be childlike is to be

perfect he was charmingly complete. His conversation was interesting to the thoughtful in the richness of the lessons he drew from common things. He would couple facts, regarded by others as unconnected, and thereby disclose unsuspected relations. It takes genius to make the rejected refuse of one generation the valuable ore of a succeeding one. This detection of a hidden meaning in the simplest matters shows the inexhaustible nature of truth, and is the mark of a superior mind".[5]

PUBLISHER'S NOTE: Permission has been granted to print the following portion of Miss Virginia Lee Cox's description of the Maury Monument soon to be erected in Richmond, Virginia:

"It is a marvelous conception of the man who was admired as the 'Pathfinder of the Seas,' and beloved for his humanity. Just how wonderful it is, is proved in the words of Commodore Maury's own daughter, Mrs. James R. Werth, who, when she saw the finished figure of Mr. Sievers' skill, said: 'I feel as if I am sitting in the presence of my father in flesh, blood, and spirit; I feel as if I could put my arms around his neck as I did when I was a little girl.'

"The sculptor has portrayed Maury in a reminiscent attitude, listening to the voice of the storm. It has been said of him that the voice of the wind and waves was music to his ears and Mr. Sievers, with fine sympathy and originality, built on much study of the man, has succeeded in showing this.

"Above the figure of Maury, which is seated in a great chair, there is a group of figures which supports the globe. The figures represent a storm on land and sea. At one corner of the monument is an ox around which cluster the windswept figures of the farmer and his household, driven before the fury of the storm.

"At the other corner is an overturned boat and figures of women and sailors, drenched in the thundering waves of the sea. The group embraces a symbolization of the world and its natural elements. Through the allegorization three of Maury's outstanding achievements are brought well to the foreground—meteorology, hydrography, and geography.

"The storm is a meteorological disturbance, and the capsized lifeboat with its occupants amid the rolling waves is symbolic of ocean meteorology, a branch of hydrography, symbolized also in the "paths of the sea" on the globe, that naturally represent geography.

---

[5] From "Library of Southern Literature", VIII, 3440.

"On the plinth of the monument in the flattest relief are figures of fish, representing Maury's interest in the paths of the sea. The story goes that once when Maury was ill he had his son read the Bible to him each night. One night he read the eighth Psalm, and when he came to the passage— 'The fishes of the sea and whatsoever walketh through the paths of the sea'— Maury had him read it over several times. Finally he said, 'If God says there are paths in the sea I am going to find them if I get out of this bed.' Thus the Psalm was the direct inspiration for his discoveries.

"Mr. Sievers has shown Maury in a reminiscent mood, representing him at that period of his life when he had achieved his greatest discoveries. In his right hand are the pencil and the compass, and in his left hand a chart. Against his chair is the Bible, from which he drew inspiration for his explorations. The sculptor has caught amazingly the spirit of the man."—From Richmond (Va.) *Times.*

LIST OF LETTERS

(Quoted in full or in part)

INDEX